Anonymus

The Cannibal Islands

or, Fiji and its People

Anonymus

The Cannibal Islands
or, Fiji and its People

ISBN/EAN: 9783743323254

Manufactured in Europe, USA, Canada, Australia, Japa

Cover: Foto ©ninafisch / pixelio.de

Manufactured and distributed by brebook publishing software (www.brebook.com)

Anonymus

The Cannibal Islands

THE

CANNIBAL ISLANDS;

OR,

FIJI AND ITS PEOPLE.

"The dark places of the earth are full of the habitations of cruelty."—Ps. lxxiv. 20.

PHILADELPHIA:
PRESBYTERIAN PUBLICATION COMMITTEE,
1334 CHESTNUT STREET.

NEW YORK: A. D. F. RANDOLPH, 683 BROADWAY.

PREFACE.

At the present day, when interest is generally aroused in regard to the South Sea Islands, an account of the Fijians will be opportune.

In America but little is known of the people, and less of the progress of Christianity among them. Although they have frequently been visited by navigators, no popular American work on the subject has been presented to the public.

The mission established in Fiji by the English having no connection with any of our missionary stations, the information that has reached us has been vague and unsatisfactory.

For much information in regard to the character and habits of the people we are indebted to the recent work of the Reverend Messrs. Thomas Williams and James Calvert, "Fiji and the Fijians." We wish also to acknowledge our obligations to Captain Wilkes' Exploring Expedition, and Captain Erskine's "Islands of the Western Pacific."

The facts here given cannot fail deeply to interest and move the heart of the reader. We have at one view the depths of degradation to which man can sink, and the power of God's grace to raise him from these depths and transform him into a follower of Christ.

CONTENTS.

PART I.

	PAGE
CHAP. I.—THE ISLANDS.— History—Scenery—Population—White Residents—Climate........	9
CHAP. II.—THE ISLANDERS.—Race—Appearance—Hair-Dressing—Dress—Tattoo.................	18
CHAP. III.—FIJIAN CHARACTER.—Vices—Lying—Pride—Anger—Hypocrisy—Self-Control—Revenge—Theft...............................	32
CHAP. IV.—GOVERNMENT.—Rank—Chiefs—Matas—Vasus—Punishments............................	51
CHAP. V.—LANGUAGE AND LITERATURE.—Copiousness—Books—Poetry—Singing..............	61
CHAP. VI.—WOMAN IN FIJI.—Degraded—Polygamy—Infanticide—Marriage—Children—The Aged and Sick—Tangithi—Burying alive	68
CHAP. VII.—FUNERAL CEREMONIES.—Tuithakau's Burial—Graves—Victims...................	88
CHAP. VIII.—CANNIBALISM.............................	102
CHAP. IX.—WAR IN FIJI.—Declared—Armies—Forts—Battles—Peace—Weapons............	115
CHAP. X.—SOCIAL HABITS.—Houses—Food—Yaqona—Feasts—Politeness—Sports—Music—Dances—Stories—Tabu...........................	126

CONTENTS.

CHAP. XI.—Occupations.—Agriculture—Manufactures—House-Building—Canoes—Fishing 148
CHAP. XII.—Religion.—Temples—Priests—Inspiration—Gods — Future State —Witchcraft —Traditions—Flood.................................. 162

PART II.

CHAP. I.—The Mission Established.—Lakemba—Preaching—Annoyances—Congregation formed—Persecution—Trials—Mbau—Reinforcement—Printing-Press 187
CHAP. II.—Ono.—No Teacher—The Praying Heathen—Wrecked Tongans—Teacher and Books for Ono—Vatoa................................. 203
CHAP. III.—Rewa.—Mbau refuses—Rewa occupied—Illness—Viwa visited 210
CHAP. IV.—Somo-Somo.—Mission begun—Troubles—Strangling—Cannibalism—Threats—Admiral Wilkes—Tuikilakila...................... 215
CHAP. V.—Viwa.—Mbau still refuses—Viwa occupied—Verani—War............................... 223
CHAP. VI.—Lakemba.—Progress made—Another Missionary—Oneata—New Chapel. 232
CHAP. VII.—Ono.—Mr. Calvert visits Vatoa and Ono—The Work prospers—Christians in War—A Native Pastor—Baptisms by Mr. Williams—A Revival... 238
CHAP. VIII.—Rewa.—New Missionaries with the Printing-Press—Enemies and Persecutions—

CONTENTS.

	PAGE
Zoar—Steady Progress—Converts—Discouragements	248

CHAP. IX.—PROGRESS IN LAKEMBA.—The New House — Papists — Tongans — The King's Daughter—Wetasau—Conversions—Tui Nayau confesses Christ 264

CHAP. X.—ONO CONVERTED.—Book-Making—Privations—A Storm—Mission Ship 276

CHAP. XI.—REWA AND SOMO-SOMO.—Dark Days in Rewa—War—Missionaries leave Rewa—Native Teacher sent—Somo-Somo abandoned by the Missionaries 283

CHAP. XII.—VERANI.—Verani of Viwa converted —His Prayer—His Labors—Death of Mr. Hunt 294

CHAP. XIII.—MBUA AND NANDI.—Christianity enters—Persecution—A Hurricane—Spread of the Truth on Vanua Levu 306

CHAP. XIV.—PROGRESS OF THE GOSPEL.—Lakemba—Rewa—Death of Ratu Nggara—War and Peace—Converts 318

CHAP. XV.—PROGRESS.—Viwa—Mbua—Church-Building—Peace made—Converts and Schools —The Nandi Mission broken up 331

CHAP. XVI.—DAY-DAWN IN MBAU.—Cannibalism —War—Tanoa dies—Human Victims—Verani slain—Thakombau *lotus*—Success at last 346

CONCLUSION 368

ILLUSTRATIONS.

	PAGE
FIJIAN HEAD-DRESSES	21
FIJIAN HEAD-DRESSES	23
FIJIAN HEAD-DRESSES	31
FIJIAN WAR-CLUBS	115
MUSICAL INSTRUMENTS	142
COCOANUT TABU	146
FIJIAN POTTERY	153
HOUSES OF FIJI	155
FIJIAN CANOE	159
MBURE, OR TEMPLE OF NA TAVASARA	162
SACRED STONES	168
FIJIAN WAR-CLUBS	223
FIJIAN WAR-CLUBS	283
MBAU	346

THE CANNIBAL ISLANDS.

CHAPTER I.

THE ISLANDS.

AFAR off in the Pacific lie the Fiji Islands, so remote from us and so unknown to us that they seem almost to belong to another world.

Every child at school learns that these islands form part of Oceanica, that they belong to the division "Polynesia," and are inhabited by a race of dark, savage cannibals. But here all information ceases. We have histories of other countries, and of the events which have brought them to their present condition; but who will tell us aught concerning the past history of the Fiji Islands? They have been settled for centuries. We know the changes in Europe, in our own land, and in most of the world, during that time. We know how republics have succeeded kingdoms, and empires republics.

But what corresponding changes have taken place among the Fijians? They are silent when we ask them of the past. How should they know? The old men are dead, and they left no records. The slight knowledge they have is so mixed with absurd stories of eight-headed gods and underground giants, that it is impossible to separate truth from falsehood. We are obliged to content ourselves with the present, judging that the antecedents of a people so degraded could present few facts either interesting or valuable.

But here are the islands, preserving traces of creation when all that God made was "good," although their inhabitants have so long served Satan that the image of God seems wellnigh blotted from their souls.

It is useless to attempt to paint in words the scenery of these islands, resting peacefully within lagoons of still, dark waters, encircled by white coral reefs, beyond which the ocean surges and roars; the mountains, their rugged tops rising dark and massive above the hills, which are glorious in tropical wealth of tangled vines and shrubs; the palm and banana, the plume-crowned cocoa-nut, the pandanus, disdaining all aid from roots, resting on prop-like branches; the ferns making an endless variety of feathery green; the gay flowers and brilliant birds. Words can give but a vague idea of the peculiar beauty of a South Sea island.

Vulanga presents a singular appearance in the group. It consists of a single mountain, the centre of which is apparently blown out, leaving a rim of broken and picturesque rocks surrounding a lake of dark-blue water, on which repose miniature isles of mossy green. A lake is also found in Somo-somo; but it is on the highest peak of the mountain, and is lost among the clouds. It is probable that this lake has formed in the place of an extinct volcano.

Many of the other islands present different and more beautiful scenery. It is evident that most of them were originally volcanic.

At present, however, the volcanoes are extinct; but their influence is still felt in occasional earthquakes and seen in the boiling springs.

The two largest islands in the group are Vanua Levu—" Great Land,"—and Na Viti Levu, or, Great Fiji. The first is more than one hundred miles long and twenty-five broad. It is noted as being the only place in these islands where sandal-wood can now be obtained. Na Viti Levu is of a different shape, being about ninety miles in length and fifty in width. It presents some of the finest landscape scenery to be found among the islands. Close to Na Viti Levu is the small low island of Mbau. It is separated from its neighbor by a low flat of coral, which is fordable even at high water and at low tide is nearly dry. Mbau is inferior to many of the other islands in size and in natural advantages, but its chief, Thakombau, now occupies a position of political power superior to that of any other in the group. It is very thickly settled, and presents a singular appearance, with its numerous thatched

THE ISLANDS.

roofs, from among which the high temples stand prominently forth. Somo-somo, Vuna, near to Mbau, Lakemba, a large, round island to the east of the others, and Ovalau, the principal residence of the white settlers, with Mbau, are the ruling powers.

The islands number, in all, about two hundred and twenty-five: of these but eighty are inhabited. The others are frequently visited for fishing-purposes, and to obtain biche-de-mar, or sea-slug, a fish which is an important article in the trade with foreign vessels. The islands lie between latitudes 15° 30′ and 20° 30′ S. and longitudes 177° E. and 178° W., covering about forty thousand square miles of the Pacific. The population is given at 150,000, Na Viti Levu alone having 50,000 inhabitants. But in the Fiji, as in the Sandwich Islands, the population is yearly diminishing, some of the smaller islands in the last fifty years having been entirely depopulated, while in the larger the decrease is manifest.

The Fiji Islands were discovered in 1643 by Abel Jasman, a Dutch navigator. After that time they were unvisited until Captain Cook, passing them, touched at one of the most remote, which he named Turtle Island, but which is better known as Vatoa. They were subsequently visited by various navigators, but little was known of them, save from the traders in sandal-wood and biche-de-mar.

Now, however, our knowledge of them is much extended, since we have accounts from British and French navigators, from the United States Exploring Expedition under Captain (now Admiral) Wilkes, in 1840, and particularly from the recent work of the Wesleyan missionaries.

In 1804, a company of twenty-seven convicts escaped from New South Wales, and fled to Fiji for liberty and license. This desperate band settled at Mbau and Rewa, where, free from all restraint, they went into such excesses as to astonish even the natives, vile as they were. The chiefs, however, were glad to secure the co-operation of the whites on the easy terms of allowing them unlimited power over the persons and property of the common people. Their superior knowledge, and the mysterious firearms, which to the Fijians appeared supernatural, might easily have secured to them absolute dominion over the islands, had their ambition led them to seek empire; but they were indifferent to every thing except the indulgence of their indolence and evil passions.

The most influential among them were Savage and Conner. Savage appears to have been the least debased and most humane among them; yet by the natives, whom he oppressed in common with his comrades, he was completely detested, and when, after nine years' residence among them, he was accidentally drowned, they rescued his remains, and, contrary to their usual custom of not eating white men, they held a grand cannibal feast over his body.

Conner lived at Rewa, where he exerted an influence equal to that of Savage at Mbau. In the days when his power was unlimited, the exercise of it was fearful. Mr. Williams says that to the influence of these two men is owing the present superiority of Mbau and Rewa,—the former having long been the most powerful state in Fiji.

The present white residents form a very influential class. Although generally extremely ignorant themselves, they are anxious to have their children educated. For this object, the missionaries now have a schoolmaster from England stationed with them at Ovalau.

Besides the advantages of trade and an easy, indolent life, there is much in the climate and beauty of these isles to tempt the sailor to tarry among them. To the educated man the objects of interest differ so much from those in his own land that the novelty is in itself a charm.

Some of the most beautiful specimens of coral formation are found here. Stretching along the shore, the reefs encircle groups of islands, making the scene peculiarly beautiful, and forming safe harbors for vessels. Yet they make navigation both difficult and dangerous; and many a brave ship, sailing over the smooth water, ignorant of the hidden reef, has suddenly struck and gone down.

Although the islands lie within the tropics, the heat is so tempered by breezes from the ocean that at certain seasons the climate is delightful; but the native dreads the season of the north winds, the *takalau*, which rarefy the air to a most painful degree during their continuance. On the leeward side of the islands the vegetation appears burnt and dying from the excessive heat and lack of moisture; but on the windward side the clouds are arrested in their progress, and give abundant and refreshing showers, making the rich tropical foliage put on its most luxuriant hue. In this latitude there are, of course, periodical rains, succeeded by long seasons of clear skies. The rainy season is from October to April. In Mr. Williams's journal is a record of a rain lasting forty-five days, which was preceded by one of twenty-four, with the brief interval of three or four clear ones.

CHAPTER II.

THE ISLANDERS.

FAR from any mainland, the Fijians hold intercourse only with the Tongans, who are their nearest island-neighbors. We may wonder from what country and how the Fijians came to these islands, and of what race they are; but our conjectures are met by the Fijian himself with a careless laugh. Why should he care where he came from? He is there. Each one has his own story to tell of the origin of mankind in general and of the Fijian in particular. If we are curious to learn something of their traditions, it may be well to listen; but, if we wish to gain knowledge, we had best turn to other sources of information.

The islands of the South Pacific are peopled by two distinct races, the Malayo-Polynesian and the Papuan. The Polynesian is of a light-yellow or copperish color, the Papuan is black. The hair of the former is long and straight, the latter short and frizzled. There are many other points of difference; but these are sufficient to show how unlike they are. To which of these do the Fijians belong? To neither, exclusively. The people of the various islands around them plainly belong to one of the two races; but in the Fijian their traits meet and mingle, showing that he is descended from both.

Their complexions vary considerably. Some of them are very dark, while others are light. Their hair is curled; but whether it would have been so had the dressing been left to nature, it is impossible to decide. They are tall and well formed. The chiefs, particularly, present a fine, muscular appearance; and many of the women are remarkable for beauty and grace.

The face is oval; the mouth large, sometimes negro-like in form, but often thin-lipped; the teeth are white and regular, the nose straight, with full nostrils; the eye is black, quick, and penetrating, and the expression of countenance intelligent and sagacious. Occasionally albinos (white-skinned persons) are seen, but not often. They suffer much from the heat of the sun, and keep their light eyes half closed through the day, unable to bear the glare.

The Queen of Rewa is described as having been a most beautiful woman, and as still retaining traces of her beauty. The following description of her half-brother, Thakombau, of Mbau, is not without parallel among them, for many of the chiefs are extremely handsome. Captain Erskine, who met him, says,—

"It was impossible not to admire the appearance of the chief: of large, almost gigantic size, his limbs were beautifully formed and proportioned; his countenance, with far less of the negro cast than among the lower orders, agreeable and intelligent; while his immense head of hair, covered and concealed with gauze, smoke-dried and slightly tinged with brown, gave him altogether the appearance of an Eastern sultan. No garments confined his magnificent chest and

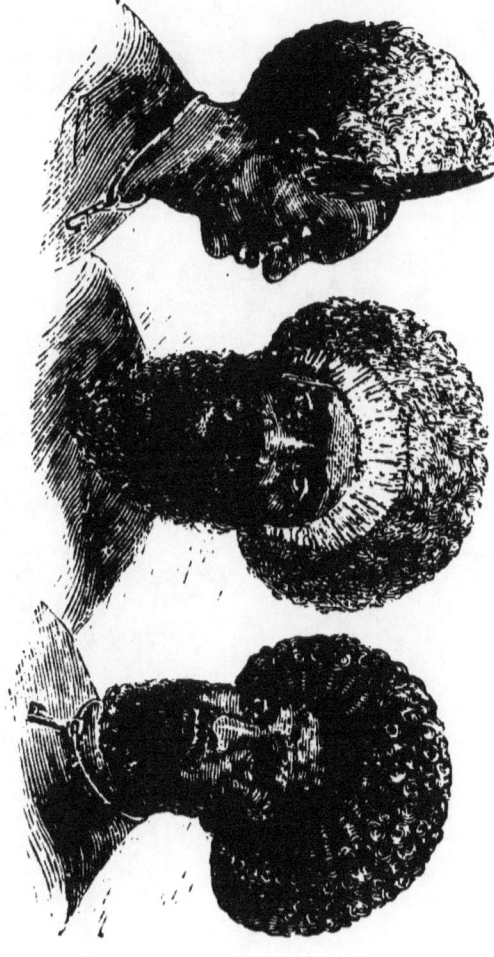

Fijian Head Dresses.

neck, or concealed the natural color of the skin,—a clear but decided black; and, in spite of this paucity of attire,—the evident wealth which surrounded him showing that it was a matter of choice and not of necessity, —he looked 'every inch a king.'"

The most striking part of the Fijian's appearance is his enormous head of hair, which to him is an object of untiring and intense interest.

We wonder at the ladies of former times, who on grand gala-days submitted with patience to the tedious operation of having their hair dressed in imitation of baskets of fruit and flowers. We laugh at the Scottish ladies who, when King George IV. visited Holyrood, were so anxious to have their heads fashionably dressed, that they yielded them to the hands of the busy barber days before the court reception.

But here we find the savage Fijian undergoing the same trouble and inconvenience, not for a week or a few days, but throughout his whole life. Every chief keeps a full complement of barbers. These are persons of importance and dignity, their hands being sacredly devoted to their master's head. They never feed themselves. Captain Hudson saw a barber of the King of Rewa drinking his ava, which was held to his lips by an attendant. His cigar was lighted and placed in his mouth by a servant's hand, and all his wants cared for in the same manner.

The operation of dressing the chief's hair is a laborious one. The barber first anoints the hair with oil, generally mixed with black, though sometimes with fancy colors. He then takes a long tortoise-shell pin, and twitches every hair till they all stand upright; then he carefully singes the whole, so that it assumes a wonderful regularity of outline. "Some heads are finished nearly like an English counsellor's wig. In some the head is a spherical mass of jet-black hair, with a white roll in front, as broad as the hand; or, in lieu of this, a white oblong occupies the length of the forehead, the black passing down on each side. In either case the black projects farther. Not a few

Fijian Head Dresses

Page 25.

are so ingeniously grotesque as to appear as if done purposely to excite laughter. One has a large knot of fiery hair on his crown, all the rest of the head being bald. Another has the most of his hair cut away, leaving three or four rows of small clusters, as if his head were planted with small paint-brushes. A third has his head bare, except where a large patch projects over each temple. One, two, or three cords of twisted hair often fall from the right temple, a foot or eighteen inches long. Some men wear a number of these braids, so as to form a curtain at the back of the neck, reaching from one ear to the other. A mode that requires great care has the hair wrought into distinct locks, radiating from the head. Each lock is a perfect cone, about seven inches long, having the base outwards; so that the surface of the hair is marked out into a great number of small circles, the ends being turned in, in each lock, towards the centre of the cone. The violent motions of the dance do not disturb these elaborate preparations; but great care is taken to preserve them from the effects of the dew or rain."

The circumference of this mass is often three feet, and sometimes five.

As lying on this extensive arrangement would destroy it, and oblige the chief to have it renewed every day, he uses a small wooden stool, which he places under his neck, regardless of the large lumps raised by it.

When he travels, he carries his stool with him. These stools are in use in many of the Pacific Islands, but are generally carved to fit the neck. The Fijian makes his simply of a round stick or log, supported by curved legs.

The hair of the boy is kept short, to make it grow more abundantly. Great pains are taken by the mother to spread it out and prepare it for the grand toilet of manhood.

The hair of the girl is allowed to grow, and when dressed it falls around the head and over the eyes like a mop. Married women wear their hair in the same style as the men, but less in size. They are not allowed to use the black powder, but generally substitute red.

The barbers are very expert in making wigs, which defy detection, when a chief is obliged thus to supply his deficiency of hair.

The dress of the people consists of a turban and *masi* or sash. The turbans are from four to six feet in length, of a thin, gauze-like material, generally smoke-colored. They last but a short time; and the chiefs, therefore, keep a large supply on hand, neatly folded, in lengths of fifteen inches and about an inch broad. The turban is of great importance, and is worn by all Fijians of respectability, excepting such as are forbidden its use. It is wrapped around the head, and fastened either in front, on the top, or at the side, in a neat bow. King Tanoa, the father of Thakombau, wore a very large and full one, coming down over the forehead to the eyes and hanging in heavy folds on the right side. Some young chiefs of taste wrap it lightly around the head and allow the long ends to float down the back.

In their dress, scanty as it is, the Fijians

display great care and pride. In judging of this matter it is very difficult for a civilized stranger to form a right opinion, influenced as he must be by the conventionalities of costume to which he is accustomed. It must be borne in mind that the character of the climate and the quality of their skin both render dress, as far as mere utility is concerned, unnecessary: the people, therefore, ought to receive full credit for modesty in the partial covering which they adopt, and about the use of which they are scrupulously particular.

The dress of the men is a kind of sash of white, brown, or figured *masi*, varying in length from three to a hundred yards. Six or ten yards, however, is the usual measure. This sash is passed between the legs, and wound two or three times round the loins, securing one end in front, so as to fall over to the knees like a curtain; the end behind is fastened in a bunch, or left to trail on the ground.

The dress of the women consists of a *liku*, or fringed band, worn around the waist.

THE ISLANDERS.

It is beautifully braided from bark, fibre, or grass, with a fringe from three to ten inches deep. The *liku* is tied at the side,—the ends on holidays being sufficiently long to form a train.

The Fijian is very fond of ornaments. Flowers, beautifully formed into wreaths and chaplets, are much used for this purpose. Cocks' feathers are very frequently worn in their hair; and chiefs wear a band of hibiscus bark around their heads, in which the gay feathers of the paroquet are stuck with the gum of the bread-fruit tree.

Breast-ornaments of large pearl shells, of circular or crescent shape, or made of boars' tusks, are very common. The noblest chiefs wear beautiful orange-colored sea-shells: these are prized very highly, and often, on great occasions, are loaned by one to the other.

Both sexes wear ear-ornaments,—the women piercing but one ear, the men both. The lobe of the ear is sometimes distended to an enormous size, admitting a ring of ten inches in circumference. The ornaments are never pendent, but generally oblong, passing through the orifice. In order to make this large enough, they use pieces of wood, shell, or rolls of tapa. White and pink armlets, and others made of a black wiry root, or white cowries, ivory and shell finger-rings, knee and ankle bands with a rose-shaped knot, are much worn; ivory, tortoise-shell, dogs' teeth, bats' jaws, snake-vertebræ, native beads ground out of shells, and foreign beads of glass, are formed into necklaces, the latter being generally braided into neat bands.

In addition to this assortment, the teeth of the victims of war are worn, and highly prized. Rank is indicated by the position of the long hair pricker, or comb. The king, or great chief, wears his in front; the next in rank, a little to the side; while the common people wear theirs back behind the ear.

The women have one original method of ornamenting themselves. They dip their heads in a thick liquid, prepared from the ashes of the bread-fruit tree, till the hair is well soaked, and then, raising their heads, they allow the preparation to run down over their faces and bodies. The zigzag lines thus formed, called *ndraou*, are considered very ornamental.

The higher classes are careful to keep themselves well oiled, and at all times to present an imposing appearance; but the lower ranks are often very slovenly.

Tattooing is used principally by the females. The young women have barbed lines on their hands and fingers, while those more advanced in years ingeniously conceal their coming wrinkles by deep-blue lines. The operation is performed solely by themselves. They use a long tooth, fixed in a handle, called a *bati-ni-ngia*, dipped in a pigment consisting of charcoal and the oil of the candle-nut. The patterns are first drawn on the body; the blackened tooth is then driven in by violent blows struck with a piece of sugar-cane. The process occupies several months; but, prolonged and severe as the pain generally is, it is willingly endured, from both pride and fear. The latter feeling arises from the belief that, if they die untattooed, their own sex, armed with sharp shells, will eternally pursue them in the next world through the most frightful scenes. So strong is this superstition that, when girls die before the operation is performed, their friends frequently paint the marks on their bodies, in order to deceive the priests and gods.

The lower classes are tattooed at the age of fourteen, but women of rank not until after marriage.

In the Tonga Islands the men are tattooed instead of the women. The Fijians humorously say the reason of this reversing of the custom was, that a Tongan who was going to tell his people of the custom repeated, as he went along, so that he might not forget, "Tattoo the women, and not the men. Tattoo the women, not the men;" but, knocking his foot against a stone, he reversed the order in his pain, and carried to his people the intelligence that they were to "tattoo the men, and not the women."

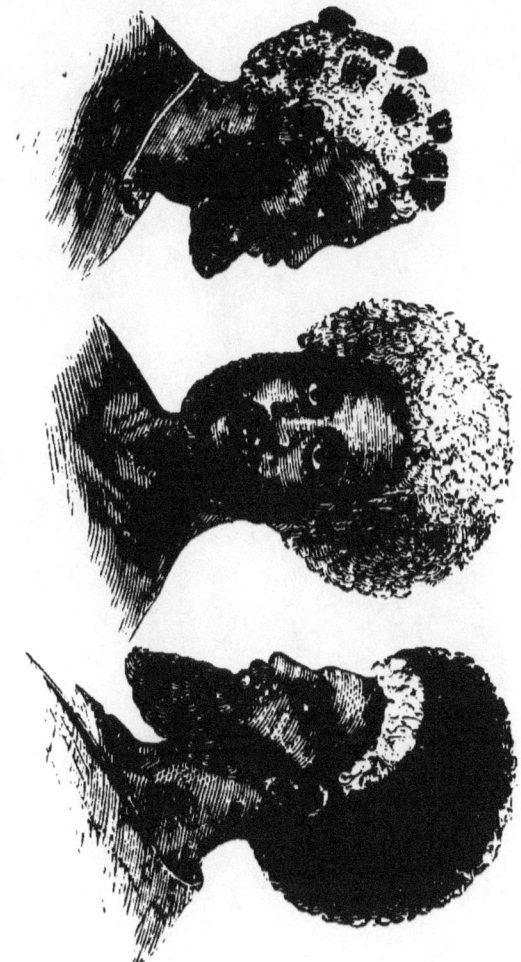

Fijian Head Dresses.

Page 31.

Both sexes paint their faces with great variety in device and color.

The Fijian, with his hair dressed in the most elaborate style, his body well oiled and face grotesquely painted, a floating train, sometimes fifty yards in length, a new turban, and his finest ornaments, desires nothing to complete his happiness but a looking-glass, and a circle of admirers around him.

CHAPTER III.

FIJIAN CHARACTER.

Intellectually the Fijian holds a high rank among the savage nations. Debased and degraded as he is, there are yet many fine points in his character which challenge our admiration and excite our sympathies. In him we find no dull, stupid savage, insensible to every thing but the indulgence of his own passions, nor, again, do we find the high mental development to which some heathen nations have attained. We see a man of quick perceptions, discriminating mind, acute feelings, of strong will, governing his passions, when he wills so to do, loyal and faithful to his friend, but the most deadly of foes to his enemy.

The Fijian's vices must be noted, to understand him as he is. Prominent among them is his pride,—a pride seen in every look and action. His personal vanity is great; and nis pride of country ranks only second to that. He is not only unwilling to think reasonably of his own truly beautiful land, but will not hear of other countries which he suspects to be in any respect superior. After Captain Wilkes pointed out Fiji on a globe to some natives, and they saw its diminutive size, they refused to look at the globe, telling their friends it was "a lying ball."

It will not, therefore, excite surprise that a travelled Fijian commands little respect from his countrymen. His superior knowledge makes him offensive to his chiefs and irksome to his equals. A Rewa man who had been to the United States was ordered by his chiefs to say whether the country of the white man was better than Fiji, and in what respects. He begged them to excuse him from speaking on that subject; but without avail. He had not gone far in telling the truth, when one cried out, "He is a prating fellow;" another, "He is impudent." Some said, "Kill him! It is natural that a foreigner should thus speak, but unpardonable in a Fijian." The luckless traveller, finding his opinions so little relished, made a hasty retreat, leaving his enraged betters to cool down at leisure.

Nothing will offend a Fijian more quickly than a slight. If the suffering individual is a woman, she will sit down,—the more public the place the better,—and sigh, sob, and whine, until she gets a good start, when she will trust to the strength of her lungs to let every one within hearing know that one of their species is injured. A reflection on a woman's character, her rank, her child, her domestic qualifications, or any one of a hundred other things, gives sufficient occasion for a wearisome cry. Nor is this demonstration restricted to females: men adopt it also. "I once," says a missionary, "saw four villages roused, and many of the inhabitants under arms, in consequence of a man crying in this style:—'War! war! Will no one kill me, that I may join the shade of my father? War! war!' This was the cry which, one clear day, sounded with singular distinctness through the air, and drew many beside myself to the top of the hill, where we found a little Mata goaded to desperation, because his friend, without consulting him, had cut several yards from some native cloth which was their joint property. To be treated so rudely made the little man loathe life; and hence the alarm. A native of Mbau put together the frame of a house, and then applied to his friends, in due form, for help to thatch it. They readily assented; but, in the course of the conversation which ensued, a remark was made that touched the pride of the applicant, who angrily resolved to make the unfinished house a monument of his high stomach, by leaving it to rot, as it actually did, in front of my own dwelling."

Lying is much easier to them than speaking the truth: an adroit liar is highly esteemed. A Fijian understands so well this habit of his people, that, if he wishes a foreigner to speak the truth, he charges him not to speak "after the fashion of Fiji."

The universal existence of this habit is so thoroughly taken for granted, that it is common to hear, after the most ordinary statement, the rejoinder, "That's a lie," or something to the same effect, at which the accused person does not think of taking offence. Any thing marvellous, on the other hand, meets with ready credence. "Walking, with a shrewd old native for my guide, on Vanua Levu," says a missionary, "he directed my attention to some stones at the side of the path. 'These,' said he, 'mark the place where a giant was slain while I was a little boy. This stone marks where his head lay, that where his knees, and these where his feet reached.' Measuring the distance with my walking-staff, I found it twenty-five feet six inches! 'Well done, Fiji!' I shouted. The old man was startled by my incredulity, for he evidently believed the tale."

They are very ready to confess if they are detected; and the pride at having forged a good lie prevents mortification at discovery. The missionaries say the pleasure the people take in the practice is so great that they often tell an untruth when the contrary would be more to their advantage.

As truth is the basis of Christian character, it would seem that the "father of lies" has skilfully planned the utter subjugation of their souls by making this trait their ruling vice.

Mr. Williams said, "The expectation of an order to set about some difficult job often makes a man wear his arm in a sling. Another, while seeming to work with fearful exertion, is all the time careful not to strain a single muscle; and the appearance of seeking a neighbor's good while only intent on their own is shown continually."

Hardly any thing is so humiliating to them as to be betrayed into a display of anger. But, as smouldering fires are most dangerous when they break forth, so when a Fijian is surprised into an outburst of anger the sight is terrible. The rage of a civilized man in comparison with what then follows is like the tossings of a restless babe. A *savage*, fully developed, physically and morally, is exhibited. The forehead is suddenly filled with wrinkles, the large nostrils distend and smoke, the staring eyeballs grow red and gleam with terrible flashings, the mouth is stretched into a murderous and disdainful grin, the whole body quivers with excitement; every muscle is strained, and the clenched fist seems eager to bathe itself in the blood of him who has roused this demon of fury. When anger is kept continually under the curb, it frequently results in sullenness. Pride and anger combined often lead to self-destruction. A chief on Thithia was addressed disrespectfully by a younger brother: rather than live to have the insult made the topic of common talk, he loaded his musket, placed the muzzle at his breast, and, pushing the trigger with his toe, shot himself through the heart.

They are most skilful hypocrites, and can dissimulate to perfection: so that the most savage cannibal will appear to be humane and gentle before a foreigner whose esteem he wishes to gain. Captain Erskine says that while at tea at the house of Mr. Lyth, the missionary then at Wiva, Ngavindi, the chief of Mbau, came in. "He was apparently under thirty years of age, of very fine figure and proportions, and altogether of prepossessing appearance. His face was painted red; and the chief's white gauze turban covered his large head of hair. He wore no covering but the ordinary wrapper, but had a boar's tusk, nearly circular, suspended from his neck; and he carried a large flat-headed club, well battered, as if by service, about the blade, which was daubed with red ochre. He took his place with perfect ease at the table, being kindly received by Mr. and Mrs. Lyth, who presented him to us. His manners were modest and gentle; and he left us even more pleased with him than we had been with Tui Levuka."

Captain Erskine was half incredulous when he was told that this man was notorious for ferocity and savage cruelty, and an active participator in the awful cannibal scenes at Mbau when the Mbutoni visited Mbau to pay their tribute.

In social diplomacy the Fijian is very cautious and clever. That he ever paid a visit merely *en passant*, is hard to be believed. If no request leaves his lips, he has brought the desire, and only waits for a good chance to present it now, or prepare the way for its favorable reception at some other time. Rarely will he fail to read your countenance; and the case must be urgent indeed which obliges him to ask a favor when he sees a frown. The more important he feels his business, the more earnestly he protests that he has none at all; and the subject uppermost in his thoughts comes last to his lips, or is not even named; for he will make a second or even a third visit rather than risk a failure through precipitancy. If it serves his purpose, he will study difficult and peculiar characters, reserving the results for future use; if, afterwards, he wishes to please them, he will know how, and if to annoy them, it will be done most exactly.

Great command of temper, and power to conceal his emotions, are often displayed by the Fijian. Let some one, for instance, bring a valuable present to a chief from whom he seeks a favor, it will be regarded with chilling indifference, although it is of all things what the delighted superior most wished to possess.

When Captain Wilkes was one day entertaining the Queen of Mathuata and her ladies, on one of his ships, they were in the cabin looking at engravings. The ladies seemed to be somewhat bored with the exhibition, when the queen suddenly noticed the fact, and spoke to them in an authoritative tone. They immediately brightened up, and chattered so merrily and seemed so interested that the captain asked the interpreter what they had seen that pleased them so much. "Nothing," was the reply. "The queen said, 'Why don't you seem pleased? why don't you laugh?'"

The plastic ladies took the hint, and repaid the captain for his civility with the most delighted smiles of interest and gratitude.

The conduct of Absalom towards his brother Amnon is exactly descriptive of what often happens in Fiji:—"And Absalom spake unto his brother Amnon neither good nor bad; for Absalom hated Amnon."

Mr. Williams was personally acquainted with the chief parties in the following tragedy, which serves to illustrate the characteristic just noted. Tui Wainunu, the principal actor, was himself his informant. In the year 1851, his cousin Mbatinamu of Mbau was slain. Shortly after Mbatinamu's death, part of a tribe from the district where he fell visited Tui Wainunu with a present of pottery, and were entertained by him for several days. One day when the party from Na Mbuna were conversing with Tui Wainunu, their chief, ignorant of their entertainer's connection with Mbau, mentioned Mbatinamu, saying that he was a fine young chief. Tui Wainunu's suspicions were at once excited, and he, pretending entire ignorance of the deceased chief, made several inquiries about him. This had the desired effect. The Mbuna chief gave Mbatinamu's history, concluding thus :—" I struck him to the earth, and was deaf to his entreaties for life." After describing how the corpse lay, he added, "I turned it upon its back, cut out the tongue by the roots, and ate it myself! And see this cord, by which my chest-key is suspended from my neck; it was braided of the ornamental tufts of hair cut from his head." "And did you eat his tongue?" calmly asked the listener. "Yes," was the reply, "I killed him, and ate his tongue." The guest was already a dead man in Tui Wainunu's estimation, but the execution of his vengeance was deferred until the eve of his visitor's departure. Then, after midnight, Tui Wainunu called around him a few trusty men and walked with them to the house where the victims slept. A blow on the wall, from the chief's heavy club, woke the inmates, who, before they could recover from their surprise, were ordered out to die, while the wrathful avenger cried, "And can you fly, that you will escape from me?" The first who came out was placed in the custody of an attendant. The next fell with his skull smashed, and the next, and the next, until eleven dead or dying men lay at the feet of the executioners. Two women of the party were kept as slaves, and the man who came out first managed to escape in the confusion. All the rest, without the slightest warning, were suddenly butchered, and their bodies shared and eaten by the friends of Tui Wainunu, who "spake" to his ill-fated guest "neither good nor bad."

Like most savages, the Fijians are covetous. To gratify this propensity they are most adroit thieves. It is not improper to steal from a neighbor, and to steal from a "papalangi," or foreigner, is highly commendable. They consider themselves privileged to appropriate any article they wish, belonging to the missionaries. They visit the mission-house, and many of them rarely go away without carrying off a memento, in the shape of some domestic utensil, stowed snugly away under the voluminous folds of their *masi*. Sometimes the families are left without tea-kettle, iron pots, or chinaware. If they find out where the articles are, the thief will laugh, and let the owners take them away.

Chiefs employ men to thieve professionally; but this is kept secret, for, if the theft be discovered, no one is more ready to punish the culprit than his employer, as by so doing he effects a threefold object,—he appears to discountenance the practice, satisfies the injured party, and chastises the thief for his unskilfulness.

Captain Wilkes speaks of a Rewa chief who told Captain Hudson that he wished very much to send his daughters to the mission-school, but could not, because the servants there were such outrageous thieves. The fact was that the servants were supplied by this same chief with special instructions to steal whatever they could for him!

It makes no difference to them whether they know the use of the articles: if they have them, that is sufficient. If they want to steal any thing from aboard ship, and it is too large to conceal, they slily drop it overboard, and when the ship has gone a diver will bring the article up for the thief.

"A brave man when not surrounded by enemies," is a native proverb which, unhappily, describes their bravery too well. But it is almost impossible for a nation so completely under the power of a chief's whims, and holding that treachery is preferable to open warfare, to be susceptible of any real courage.

One of their most striking traits is their never-sleeping vengeance for real or fancied insults. Not only their personal injuries, but an insult to their family, friends, or their tribe, calls forth the same untiring endurance of difficulties, dangers, and privations for the sake of revenge. Sometimes a row of sticks or stones is placed in the ground to remind the owner of his injuries, and they are carefully preserved till he has obtained complete satisfaction.

Sometimes a man is seen with the exact half of his head closely cropped, to which disfigurement another will add a long twist of hair hanging down the back; and thus they will appear until they have wreaked vengeance on those who slew their wives while fishing on the reef. From the ridgepole of some chief's house, or a temple, a roll of tobacco is suspended; and there it must hang until taken down to be smoked over the dead body of some one of a hated tribe. A powerful savage, of sober aspect, is seen keeping profound silence in the village council. To ordinary inquiries he replies with a whistle. His son, the hero of the village, fell by a treacherous hand, and the father has vowed to abstain from the pleasures of conversation until he opens his lips to revile the corpse of his son's murderer or to bless the man who deprived it of life. Irritating songs are employed to excite the hatred of those who are likely to let their vengeance sleep. The youths of the place assemble before the house, and *leletaka*, or lament, that none revenge the death of their friend. The effect of such a song, framed so as to appeal to the most sensitive points of the Fijian's nature, is to awaken the malice and fury of those to whom it is addressed with all their original force, and vows of bloody retribution are made afresh.

Fijians express their malice in strong

terms. "My hatred of thee begins at the heels of my feet, and extends to the hairs of my head." An angry chief sent the following message to the object of his displeasure: "Let the shell of the *vasua*" (the giant oyster) "perish by reason of years, and to these add a thousand more; still my hatred of thee shall be hot!" This relentless animosity will pursue its object to the grave, and gratify itself by abusing a putrid carcass.

An illustration is given by Mr. Williams in the case of Nalila and Ngvindi, the chief whose "modest and gentle manners" were accepted by Captain Erskine as an index to his character. Nalila was condemned to death, but for several years escaped by living in strict seclusion on an island where he was safe from pursuit. Despairing at last of capturing him, his foes made overtures of peace, which were accepted, and he returned to Mbau. On the second day of his return he sat with them and some of his personal friends around the yaqona-bowl, in a gay humor, when suddenly a shot from outside laid him dead. Ngvindi sprang to his feet with his heavy club uplifted to crush him as he had fallen. Nalila's father interposed and begged him to have mercy, but his only answer was a blow which stretched him a corpse by his son. The heart, liver, and lungs of Nalila were eaten by his late companions; then they "gave up the mutilated body to the tears of his widow," who no doubt was strangled in accordance with their usual customs, and the revenge of Ngvindi's party was satisfied.

Dark are these pictures of savage cruelty, of brutality and cannibalism; and a volume of such pictures can be given by the missionaries who have dwelt in Fiji. How low man can sink, and how low he will sink without the Bible, we here learn. It is this one thing that makes the Fijian to differ from the Christian American. God has given us his word and has brought to us the knowledge of Jesus Christ. By this have we risen from the degradation and the idolatry of our ancestors, who, centuries ago, were savage heathen in Britain, Germany, or France. By this same power even Fijians have been transformed, and thousands of these once cannibal savages are now the followers of Christ.

CHAPTER IV.

GOVERNMENT.

In Fiji each island has its own chief or king. The weaker rulers, however, acknowledge the supremacy of more powerful ones. Mbau, Somosomo, Lakemba, and Rewa, are the four great powers in Fiji.

Society is divided into six classes, each perfectly distinct from the others. They are—

1. Kings and queens.
2. Chiefs of large islands or districts.
3. Chiefs of towns, priests, and mata-nivanuas.
4. Distinguished warriors of low birth, chiefs of the carpenters, and chiefs of the fishers for turtle.
5. Common people.
6. Slaves by war.

The power of the king is unlimited, and his authority absolute. The character of the government, therefore, varies with the king's. When the succession is regular, it descends to the late king's eldest brother, then to the eldest son of the king, then to the son of the eldest brother. There are many circumstances, however, that influence the succession. The rank of the mother is one. If she is not of noble birth, her son is deprived of all right. Then the king often exercises his prerogative of putting his heir to death, or an ambitious subject, believing that might is right, will seize the crown.

The dignity of the office is fully realized,— so much so that republicanism is held in contempt by the Fijians, and even the United States have a king when American citizens speak of their President to a native of the islands.

The pride of the kings is often amusing. They do not scruple to call themselves gods, demanding and receiving reverence as such. Mr. Williams, in speaking of the sacredness of the king's person and every thing he touches, says,—

"Hence arise some amusing scenes. A

poor man was ordered to carry a chair on which Tuithakau was accustomed to sit: he first encased the palms of his hands with green leaves, then, taking the chair by two of its legs, lifted it above his head to avoid further contact, and ran off at full speed, as though in so doing lay his only chance of completing the journey alive. One day, on leaving the house of the same chief, I held in my hand a ripe plantain, which I gave to a child outside; but an old man snatched it away with a countenance expressive of as much anxiety as if I had given the child a viper. His fear was that the fruit had been touched by the king, and would therefore cause the child's death. This king took advantage of his hallowing prerogative in an odd way. He used to dress an English seaman in his *masi* (dress), and send the man to throw the train over any article of food, whether dead or alive, which he might happen to come near. The result was that such things were at once conveyed to the king without a word of explanation being required."

The cares and duties of a king in Fiji are not onerous. His principal occupations are feasting and fighting. He is one day receiving the homage of his subjects in royal state, the next will find him hard at work in his garden or sitting in his house plaiting sinnet, or, like old Sanoa, lying indolently before a fire, sleeping away half his time. He has several attendants always in readiness to wait on him, feed him, or perform the most menial services. These, with his priest and wives, make up his retinue.

The chiefs who occupy the rank next below the kings also claim descent from the gods, and the power they exercise is arbitrary and despotic. As an instance of their mode of government, it is told that a Rewa chief wished a man to give him a hoe: this he was unwilling to do, so the chief took his wife. Whether the man felt that he was punished is doubtful, for wives are more easily obtained than hoes among them. At another time, a chief wishing to collect his people together ordered that all who refused to come should be baked!

The third class includes "chiefs of towns, priests, and mata-ni-vanuas." These petty chiefs are only distinguished from those already described by the possession of less power. The priests will be described hereafter. We therefore pass immediately to the matas, or courtiers. The title signifies "the eyes (or "the face") of the land," and their office is to communicate between the chiefs and their people. They are stationed at the several towns under their chief's control, where they act as messengers, each bearing in his title the name of the place to which he is ambassador, as "Mata ki Lakemba," "Mata ki Vatoa." They are treated with the greatest respect by the people, who are well aware of the influence of their representations.

The matas frequently have a number of messages to carry back and forth, and to assist their memory they use mnemonic sticks, corresponding in number to their messages, and of lengths varied according to the subject the message contains. When the mata delivers his message he lays down the appropriate stick, and so continues till messages and sticks are alike exhausted. "In some parts of Fiji the mata holds his post for life, in others for only a few years. In the latter case, when tired of public life, he presents a large quantity of provisions to his chief, asking for permission to retire."

On many of the islands the king has a mata attached to his person, called "O na Mata," whose duties are to address the people in his master's stead when they bring tribute or food.

Among the most curious of the Fijian customs is the institution of the "*Vasu*," a word properly meaning a nephew or niece, but which denotes an office having extraordinary privileges. A *Vasu tankei* is a title given to a nephew of the king, whose mother was a lady of rank in her home. He has the right of claiming any thing belonging to a native of his mother's land, whether king or commoner, excepting the wives, houses, and lands of the chiefs. No matter what the rank of the victim may be, he rarely resists the claim.

Captain Wilkes gave Tanoa, the father of Thakombau, and the most powerful king in the islands, a handsome rifle. As soon as his *vasu* heard of it, he resolved to have it, together with some watches which had been presented to the royal family. Some of the watches he obtained; but Tanoa, unwilling to part with his new patent rifle, sent it away for safety, although the *vasu* declared he would yet have it. This same man was at war with his uncle, and actually made this extraordinary attempt to supply himself with ammunition from his enemy's stores.

The *vasu* does not often appropriate the property of the chiefs, but contents himself with that of the people. He is of great service to the king, who sends him occasionally with a large fleet to different parts of his dominion to seize on a large amount of property and divide it with the king.

Public affairs are generally managed by the chiefs; but councils are often held. At these meetings much discretion and intelligence are exhibited. Only chiefs of age or wisdom speak; and the one who would venture to make a foolish or ill-digested speech, or propose some impracticable or ridiculous measure, would be disgraced.

Crime with the Fijians usually means an offence committed by the weaker against the stronger, who in his own way punishes the offender. Theft is punished by a "fine, repayment in kind, loss of finger, or clubbing."

At Lakemba the missionaries were robbed. Having complained formally to the king, in a few days they were waited on by a messenger from him. He brought many apologies for the offence, and five sticks, on each of which was a little finger that had been cut from one of the five culprits.

A severer punishment was inflicted on a native who stole a comb from one of the chiefs. He was placed on a canoe-mast, one end being elevated a few inches above the ground; his hands were tied above his head, and a rope was lashed around him, fastening him securely to the mast. In this condition he was left all day, exposed to the burning sun. At evening he was loosened, but he could not walk; and this most brutal punishment was said to have been *slight*, because the American ships were there.

The despotism exhibited in punishment is as astonishing as the resignation of the victim. A man is often judged in his absence, and executed before he is aware that sentence has been passed on him. If condemned to death, when the executioner comes the victim rarely questions the justice of the sentence, saying, "Whatever the king wills must be done."

Justice is known by name to the Fijian powers, and its form sometimes adopted; yet in very many criminal cases the evidence is partial and imperfect, the sentence precipitate and regardless of proportion, and its execution sudden and brutal. The injured parties, headed by the nearest chief, form the "bench" to decide the case. If the defendant's rank is higher than their own, an appeal is made to the king as chief magistrate, and this is final.

Since the establishment of Christianity in the islands, however, justice has become more than a name, and crime has begun to be properly recognized and proportionately punished. The word of God has thrown light, moral light, upon these dark places of the earth; wrong-doing is seen to be crime, and the punishment of the wrong-doer and the protection of the innocent is recognized as right. Plain as this seems to us in happier lands, it is new to Fiji.

CHAPTER V.

LANGUAGE AND LITERATURE.

In the languages of all the Oceanic islands there is a marked resemblance, but not enough to obviate the necessity of making each a separate study. The Fijian is divided into about fifteen dialects. That of Mbau may be styled the *court* language, and the missionaries wisely used it for the translation of the Bible.

Among the most striking features of the Fijian language are its copiousness and its precision. A native is exceedingly particular to express himself correctly, using terms remarkable for their accuracy and propriety.

There is a separate Fijian word for the cocoa-nut in every stage of its growth, as well as in every variety; and every shrub, flower, and tree on the islands has its own appropriate name.

According to testimony founded on a long acquaintance with the language, the Fijian can express by different words the motion of a snake and that of a caterpillar, with the clapping of the hands lengthwise, crosswise, or in almost any other way; it has three words for "a bunch," five for "a pair," six for "cocoa-nut oil," and seven for "a handle;" for "the being close together" and for "the end" it has five terms each, for "fatigue" and "thin" seven each, with no fewer than eleven for "dirty;" for the verb "to thank" it has two words, for "to pluck," four; for "to carry, command, entice, lie, raise," it has five each; for "to creep, return, pierce, see, squeeze," six each; for "to care, draw, roll," seven each; for "to make, place, push, turn," eight each; for "to seize and split," nine each; with fourteen for "to cut," and sixteen for "to strike."

One other illustration of the copiousness of the language is worth mention. The Greek and other cultivated tongues have different words for "to wash," according as the operation has reference to the body, or to clothes and the like; and, where the body is spoken of, their synonyms will sometimes define the limb or part which is the subject of the action. The Fijian leaves these languages far behind, for it can avail itself of separate terms to express the washing process, according as it may happen to affect the head, face, hands, feet, and body of an individual, or his apparel, his dishes, or his floor.

In 1840 the Fijian dictionary contained about five thousand eight hundred words; and many have since been added.

The missionaries are generally acquainted with seven of the dialects, and have translated books into four,—those of Mbau, Rewa, Lakemba, and Somosomo.

Rev. David Hazlewood, in 1850, completed a grammar and dictionary, which have proved of great service. A few useful books have since been added to the list; and they hope soon to be able to issue some school-books for the use of the children.

The translation of the Bible was commenced by Rev. John Hunt, but was left unfinished by him at his death. It was resumed by Mr. Hazlewood, who was peculiarly adapted to the difficult work. He prepared an excellent manuscript, which was carried by Mr. Calvert to England and printed by the Bible Society.

Rude and inharmonious as the poetry and songs of the Fijian seem to us, to him they are the perfection of melody. The love of the natives for their poetry amounts to a passion. Through the day all classes enliven their tasks with their peculiar chant, and at night the air resounds with the voices of numbers who have met for recitation. The glory of Fijian poetry, however, is heard in the *meke*, a term which applies to both song and dance. As the performer moves in the dance, he accompanies himself in songs, the movement of which is slow and monotonous, varied principally by alternations of the time. Beginning as slowly as a dirge, he suddenly rattles off a few notes rapidly, then relapses into his slow movement, and, after shrieking in a high tone, he stops, and the bass comes in, chanting his part on one note.

Thus alternating, they weary the ear with their dreary song.

A finished poem is unknown among them, although poetic expressions are common. Can any phrase be prettier than "*lumaluma*," which expresses both modesty and the softened retiring light of evening? Ignorance is appropriately called "the night of the mind."

The two favorite muses reside on the islands Nairai and Thekombia-i-ra. The first is a man, the other a woman; and to them the poets ascribe the influence that causes them to compose the *meke*.

They say that, while asleep, they visit the world of spirits, where a poetic divinity teaches them a poem, while, at the same time, they learn a dance corresponding to the song. The heaven-taught minstrels then return to their mundane home, and communicate the new acquisition to their friends, by whom, on their trading or festive visits, it is spread far and wide through every town and island. No alteration is ever made in the *meke*, however the language may differ from the dialect of the people among whom it is introduced: hence the natives are often ignorant of the meaning of many of their most popular songs, and express surprise if any one should expect them to understand them.

Some of the native Christians have composed hymns that are quite creditable. The following song is a fair specimen of ordinary Fijian poetry:—

" In Rewa a fine southerly wind was blowing,
  The wind was blowing from the point of Rewa,
  And it shakes down the garlands of the sinu-tree,
  So that the women may make garlands.
  String the sinu, and cover it with the lemba flowers;
  When put together, I will hang it on my neck.
  But the Queen begs it, and I will take it off;
  Queen! take our garland of lemba.
  I throw it on the little couch.
  Take ye the garland that I have been making,
  That the ladies may make a great noise in coming.
  Let us go to the Thungraiva [a house].
  The mother of Thangi-lemba was vexed.
  Why did you give away our dance
  The basket of dance-fees is empty.
  This world is a world of trouble.
  They will not succeed in learning to dance.
  The sun goes down too soon in Muthuata."

The people now sing the Te Deum and other parts of public worship to their native chants. The music is not unpleasing, and is said to resemble the chanting in a Jewish synagogue.

CHAPTER VI.

WOMAN IN FIJI.

We shall be sadly disappointed if we expect to find among these people the domestic habits and the love of home common to more civilized nations. The rigid enforcement of unnatural customs—as *tabuing* parents and children, brothers and sisters, from speaking to each other, forbidding a father to speak to a son over fifteen years of age, or a husband to eat from the same dish with his wife, and many similar rules—prevents this. We could hardly expect a man to find his chief pleasure in one room of a reed-thatched house with a dozen or more wives and children chattering and quarrelling around him.

Their carelessness of manner is generally the expression of real indifference. The women are considered as a kind of property, and are of importance only when related to a chief. In many of the islands they are beasts of burden; and in all of them the whole sex is fearfully degraded. They are at the mercy of their husbands and friends, who can dispose of or use them as they choose; but among natives themselves women are not, as has been sometimes asserted, an article of trade. If they are ever treated in this way, it is brought about by white men. An American captain once asked two hogs as the price of a musket. The chief, who desired to purchase it, had but one hog: so he sent with it a woman, hoping the *papalangi* would think her worth as much as the missing animal. She was received as an equivalent; and the wife of the captain, liking the woman, kept her for a servant.

The system which permits a plurality of wives necessarily produces the most terrible results. Quarrelling and jealousy are among the lesser evils.

Mr. Williams thus represents the harem of a chief:—"The testimony of a woman who lived two years in my family, after having been one among several of a chief's wives, is, that they know nothing of comfort. Contentions among them are endless, the bitterest hatred common, and mutual cursing and recrimination of daily occurrence. When a woman happens to be under the displeasure of her master as well as that of his lady wives, they irritate the chief by detailing her misdemeanors, until permission is gained to punish the delinquent, when the women of the house—high and low—fall upon her, cuffing, kicking, scratching, and even trampling on the poor creature, so unmercifully as to leave her half dead." And the end of this life commonly is the privilege of forming one of the number strangled at the chief's funeral. Darkness and degradation are the lot of woman where God's precious gospel is unknown. In Fiji heathenism casts its deepest gloom over the lives and characters and fills with wretchedness the fortunes of those who in Christian lands are examples of piety and of all that is refined and amiable.

It is hardly possible to expect from a mother, under these circumstances, either devoted or judicious affection; and yet a good measure of maternal fondness is often shown. Often the first act of the Fijian mother is to murder her child. To such an extent is infanticide carried, that murderesses by profession are to be found in nearly every village. But the mother's hand is often the nearest and readiest. Unlike the infanticide of the Hindus, that of Fiji is done from motives in which there is no admixture of any thing like religious feeling or fear, but merely whim, expediency, anger, or indolence. If the babe is a female, her chances of life are considerably lessened.

In the exercise of his authority, the husband is often cruel. The use of the stick he finds frequently necessary to subdue an unruly wife. Mr. Williams saw sticks the size of a broom-handle, that the kings of Lakemba and Mbau kept by their sides for this purpose.

"The aged king Tuithakau II.," says Mr. Williams, "visited me one day in evident trouble. After sitting silent a while, he said, 'Have you a spy-glass?' Finding that I had one, he proceeded, 'Do look, and see if my woman has gone to Weilangi only, or right away to Wainikeli.' Weilangi was a village about six miles off, and Wainikeli about six miles farther, with high hills interposed. It appeared that the old gentleman had found it necessary to use severe discipline with one of his wives, who, after being beaten, ran away; and he now felt anxious about her, and came to solicit the help of my glass to ascertain her whereabouts. I assured him that in this case the spy-glass was of no use, as the woman had been gone several hours, and was now, no doubt, in some house with her friends. 'Look,' he rejoined, 'if you can see her footsteps on the road from Weilangi to Wainikeli.' It was with difficulty that I persuaded him that it was impossible to see, at such a distance, a path which was narrow and irregular, and, moreover, hidden with forest and brushwood."

The girls are generally betrothed in infancy, and if they are of high rank the engagement is considered inviolable, as political considerations are involved. In the lower classes, however, if the man dislikes the bargain, he may neglect to make the customary advances; if the reluctance is on the woman's side, she may be released by the giving of property in her stead. It is rare to find a marriage founded on mutual esteem: yet such a one is sometimes made. The wives envy the English woman, who can wed "the man to whom her spirit flies." Yet some more ignorant natives, supposing the missionaries had bought their wives, asked them how much they gave for them.

The ceremonies connected with betrothment and marriage are numerous, and carefully observed among the higher classes. Priests are not in requisition for a marriage, as it is a civil and not a religious contract.

The girl's friends take her to the house of her intended husband's parents, presenting, at the same time, property,—teeth, cloth, or mats. A custom which is certainly pretty is then observed. Not even a heathen can leave the scenes of childhood and careless joy without tears; and the girl often weeps freely. The friends of the bridegroom endeavor to solace her by presenting trinkets as expressions of their regard. This is called the *vakamamaca,* or "drying-up-of-the-tears." This, however, is not the end of the ceremony. The bride returns to her home after the observance of certain forms.

The young man is expected to build a house to which to take his wife, who undergoes now the painful process of tattooing, if it has not already been done. During this period the bride is *tabu siga,* kept from the sun, to improve her complexion. These preliminaries over, the grand feast takes place, when the friends of each party try to outdo the others in the food and property presented. As in other native feasts, so here it is easier to specify the good cheer by yards and hundred-weights than by dishes. When the chief Tanoa gave his daughter to the Lasakau chief, there was provided for the entertainment of the friends assembled a wall of fish five feet high and twenty yards in length, besides turtles and pigs, and vegetables in proportion. One *dish* at the same feast was ten feet long, four feet wide, and three deep, spread over with green leaves, on which were placed roast pigs and turtles. Whatever is prepared by the friends of the woman is given to those of the man, and *vice versâ*. The conclusion of this day is the *vaqasea*, when the marriage is complete, the announcement of which, in some tribes, is by tremendous shoutings; and arrangements are made for the *veitasi*, or "clipping," which, to windward, consists in cutting off a bunch of long hair worn over the temples by the woman while a spinster. To leeward, however, the woman is deprived of all her hair, and thus made sufficiently ugly to startle the most ardent admirer.

The bride, among the higher classes, has nothing to say on the subject, her will being too unimportant to be consulted. Suitability in age is of no consequence, as young girls of sixteen are often married to men of sixty.

Says Mr. Williams, "I saw a young girl of good family, who was given to the daughter of Tuikilakila, brought in form to that chief. As she was presented in the way usually observed in giving a bride, I will describe the ceremony. She was brought in at the principal entrance by the king's aunt and a few matrons, and then, led only by the old lady, approached the king. She was an interesting girl of fifteen, glistening with oil, wearing a new *liku*, and a necklace of carved ivory points, radiating from her neck, and turning upwards. The king then received from his aunt the girl, with two whales' teeth, which she carried in her hand. When she was seated at his feet, his majesty repeated a list of their gods, and finished by praying that 'the girl might live, and bring forth male children.' To her friends—two men who had come in at the back door—he gave a musket, begging them not to think hardly of his having taken their child, as the step was connected with the good of the land, in which their interests, as well as his own, were involved. The musket, which was about equivalent to the necklace, the men received with bent heads, muttering a short prayer, the close of which was exactly the same as they had offered for years, 'Death to Natawa!' Tuikilakila then took off the girl's necklace, and kissed her. The gayest moment of her life, as far as dress was concerned, was past; and I felt that the untying of that polished ornament from her neck was the first downward step to a dreary future. Perhaps her forebodings were like mine, for she wept; and the tears were seen by the king, who said, 'Do not weep. Are you going to leave your own land? You are but going a voyage, soon to return. Do not think it is a hardship to go to Mbau. Here you have to work hard; there you will rest. Here you fare indifferently; there you will eat the best of food. Only do not weep to spoil yourself.' As he thus spoke, he played with her curly locks, complimenting her on her face and figure. Just then the king's women appeared with their nets, and he ordered the poor girl to go and 'try her hand at fishing.'"

The birth of a boy is hailed with feasting and rejoicing. The child is anointed with oil and turmeric, and is named when two or three days old.

The first lesson taught a child is to strike its mother,—to make it courageous. For the same object mothers take their little ones to abuse the dead bodies of their fathers' enemies. One of the missionaries, visiting a family who were mourning the recent slaughter of six of their household, saw a child of about four years of age sitting on the floor, hacking a *malo*—a man's dress—with a butcher's knife. His little hand was covered with blood, for his little finger had been cut off as a token of love for his deceased father. This *malo* had been stripped from one of the enemies, and given to him to treat in this way, for the purpose of exciting hatred and revenge.

The principal education of the children consists in teaching them to throw a spear or club, and manage a canoe. They also become well versed in the qualities of the natural objects around them. Captain Erskine said he never met a boy or girl who could not tell him the native name for any leaf or grass shown them.

The Fijian in no way excites our horror and pity more than in his treatment of the sick and aged. Generally, "if sick persons have no friends, they are simply left to perish. Should they be among friends, they are cared for until they become troublesome, or, through weakness, offensive; whereupon they are generally put out of the way." If the patient is of high rank, on the contrary, great efforts are frequently made to preserve his life.

The case of Tangithi is a good illustration of their habits in this respect. She was the favorite daughter of the king of Lakemba, and was very ill. She wished to be visited by the missionary, who found her speechless and apparently insensible. The medicine he gave soon produced a favorable change; but next day she refused to continue under Mr. Calvert's treatment, as a priest had arrived during the night from a distance, and, through him, the god had declared that the illness of the princess was in consequence of the ruinous state of the temples. The king, being very fond of his daughter, was anxious to appease the anger of the gods, and ordered large offerings of food to be prepared by all the towns on the island. Toki, and the other enemies of the *lotu*, tried very hard to get this order imposed on the Christians as well as the rest; but the king refused, saying that what the Christians did in the matter would be useless, as they worshipped another God. On being pressed, he added, "They shall not be asked to help. And if they were, do you think they would do any thing in this matter, seeing that such work is unlawful to them?" On this occasion, as on all others, care was taken by the missionaries that, while the Christians stood firmly to their principles, it should be done with as little offence as possible; so that they brought unbidden a supply of uncooked food, as a present to the king, who seemed pleased and satisfied. All the heathens on the island joined in preparing the offering for Tangithi's recovery.

All these preparations occupied much time, and before every thing was ready Tangithi grew worse, and again Mr. Calvert was sent for. He found her removed to the house of a late brother of the king, who was now deified, and said to be specially present in his old house. The missionary, knowing that the priest was there about his incantations, and that large offerings had been prepared, deemed this a good opportunity for teaching. The king was much excited, and said, " The illness of my daughter is very great!" "Yes," said Mr. Calvert, "I know it; and you are to be blamed for following useless heathen worship, instead of continuing the use of medicine which proved beneficial." He further added that he was unwilling to treat the patient while the heathen observances were going on, and the priest was rubbing her body, lest, on his treatment succeeding, it should be said that the recovery was the result of the incantations and offerings, and thus the people should become confirmed in their errors. After a long talk, and a lecture to the priest on his absurd deceptions, Mr. Calvert at last consented to undertake the case. He administered a stimulant, which revived the girl from her stupor, making her throw about her arms restlessly. This frightened the king, who thought she was dying, and cried out, angrily, "You have killed my daughter!" The missionary was in no enviable position. The attendants and people all round were very savage at his interference with the priest, and only wanted a word to lead them to revenge. It was late at night, and the mission-house was far off. The place was full of enraged heathens, in the midst of whom stood the stranger accused by the king of murdering his favorite child. Nothing, however, was to be gained by showing fear: so Mr. Calvert snatched up his bottles, and showed great indignation at such a charge after he had come at their earnest request,—though served so badly by them before,—and had given some of the medicine that had been sent all the way from England for his own family. Then, assuming a look of being greatly affronted, he hurried away, glad enough to get safe home, where he bolted all the doors, and kept an anxious look-out next morning, until the news came that Tangithi was alive and somewhat better. During the morning a message came from the king, begging for medicine for another of his children, who was ill with dysentery. Mr. Calvert sent word, "Give my respects to the king, and tell him that I do not wish to send any more medicine for his children, having killed his daughter last night; and it is not lawful for a missionary to kill two children of a king in so short a time." An apology soon came, and an entreaty for forgiveness for words hastily spoken; but the medicine was not sent until another urgent request was brought.

For four weeks the priests tried all the effects of their incantations and sacrifices, but the sick girl got no better: so that at last tne father's heart relented, and he gave his consent that she should renounce heathenism, and be removed, with her attendants, to the mission-house. This was accordingly done; and the missionary's wife will not soon forget the toil and inconvenience and annoyance of having so many Fijian women in her house. The care, however, was cheerfully borne, and in a short time the patient improved. Now that she had lost all trust in the heathen remedies, she was perfectly submissive to the directions of the missionary, and soon recovered. And God greatly blessed her soul as well as her body; so that she became an enlightened and earnest worshipper of him, much to the dismay of the priests and the rousing of the whole island. Several became Christians in the king's town, and all the people, from the king downwards, knew that Tangithi's recovery was of God, after their own priests had failed.

This young girl's high position alone saved her from the horrible fate that befalls those of a lower class. Elijah Verani, after becoming a Christian, one day told Mr. Williams of a young girl, who had been sick, and remained in a delicate state of health for so long a time that he feared she would be troublesome, and had her grave dug. She was in the house, but the noise and loud exclamations attracted her attention, and she went to the door to see what could be the reason of it. As soon as she appeared, she was suddenly seized, carried to her grave, and thrown in. In vain she shrieked and pleaded for mercy: two pair of strong arms held her down, resisting her frantic struggles and her agonizing cry, "Do not bury me! I am quite well now!" The soil was hastily thrown in on her, till every sound was stifled, and they left her. Oh, the horrors of heathenism! Well may we thank God for the Bible!

One reason, probably, why the sick and aged desire to die before they become decrepit, is the belief that they will eternally be of the same age that they are at the time of death. The treatment they receive also often reconciles them to death; but, if they do not themselves make the proposal, their children are very apt to remind them of their duty to die. To honor and cherish the aged is no part of Fijian morality.

Mr. Hunt, who was an eye-witness of several of these acts, gives the following account. On one occasion he was called upon by a young man, who desired he would pray to his Spirit for his mother, who was dead. On inquiry, the young man told him that his brothers and himself were just going to bury her. Mr. Hunt accompanied the young man, telling him he would follow in the procession and do as he desired him, supposing, of course, the corpse would be brought along. Soon they met the procession: the young man said this was the funeral, and pointed out his mother, who was walking along with them, as gay and lively as any present, and apparently as much pleased. Mr. Hunt expressed his surprise to the young man, and asked him how he could deceive him by saying his mother was dead, when she was alive and well. He said, in reply, that they had made her death-feast; that she was old; that his brother and himself had thought she had lived long enough, and it was time to bury her, to which she had willingly assented, and they were about it now. He had come to Mr. Hunt to ask his prayers, as they did those of the priest. He added that it was from love to his mother that they were now going to bury her, and that none but themselves could or ought to perform so sacred an office. Mr. Hunt did all in his power to prevent the act; but the only reply he received was that she was their mother, and they were her children, and they ought to put her to death. On reaching the grave, the mother sat down,—when children, grandchildren, relations, and friends took an affectionate leave of her. A rope was then passed twice around her neck by her sons, who took hold of it and strangled her; after which she was put into her grave with the usual ceremonies. They returned to feast and mourn, after which she was as entirely forgotten as though she had not existed.

CHAPTER VII.

FUNERAL CEREMONIES.

Deeply painful is it to the Christian heart to describe or to read of the horrors of heathenism in these beautiful islands. Yet it is well to know what man is without the knowledge of God, and what was the state of many who now obey the gospel. In the funeral ceremonies of Fiji we see new evidences of the cruelty and woes of pagan blindness. The story of the death and funeral of an eminent chief, Tuithakau, of Somo-somo, is thus described by Mr. Williams:—

"The venerable chieftain grew feeble towards the middle of 1845, but not so as to prevent his taking an occasional walk. About August, however, he was obliged to keep his mat, and I often called, and endeavored to instruct without irritating him. I visited him on the 21st, and was surprised to find him much better than he had been two days before. We talked a little, and he was perfectly collected. On being told, therefore, on the morning of the 24th, that the king was dead, and that preparations were being made for his interment, I could scarcely credit the report. The ominous word *preparing* urged me to hasten without delay to the scene of action; but my utmost speed failed to bring me to Nasima—the king's house—in time.

"The moment I entered it, it was evident that, as far as concerned two of the women, I was *too late* to save their lives. Scores of deliberate murderers, in the very act, surrounded me: yet there was no confusion, and, except a word from him who presided, no noise, but only an unearthly, horrid stillness. Nature seemed to lend her aid to deepen the dread effect: there was not a breath stirring in the air, and the half-subdued light in that hall of death showed every object with unusual distinctness. All was motionless as sculpture, and a strange feeling came upon me, as though I was becoming a statue. To speak was impossible; I was unconscious that I breathed; and involuntarily, or, rather, against my will, I sank to the floor, assuming the cowering posture of those who were not actually engaged in murder. My arrival was during a hush, just at the crisis of death; and to that strange silence must be attributed my emotion; for I was but too familiar with murders of this kind, neither was there any thing novel in the apparatus employed.

"Occupying the centre of that large room were two groups, the business of which could not be mistaken. All sat on the floor,—the middle figure of each group being held in a sitting posture by several females and hidden by a large veil. On either side of each veiled figure was a company of eight or ten strong men, one company hauling against the other on a white cord, which was passed twice round the neck of the doomed one, who thus in a few minutes ceased to live.

"As my self-command was returning, the group farthest from me began to move; the men slackened their hold, and the attendant women removed the large covering, making it into a couch for the victim. As that veil was lifted, some of the men beheld the distorted features of a mother whom they had helped to murder, and smiled with satisfaction as the corpse was laid out for decoration. Convulsive struggles on the part of the poor creature near me showed that she still lived. She was a stout woman, and some of the executioners jocosely invited those who sat near to have pity and help them. At length the women said, 'She is cold.' The fatal cord fell; and, as the covering was raised, I saw dead the obedient wife and unwearied attendant of the old king. Leaving the women to adjust her hair, oil her body, cover her face with vermilion, and adorn her with flowers, I passed on to see the remains of the deceased Tuithakau. To my astonishment, I found him alive! He was weak, but quite conscious, and, whenever he coughed, placed his hand on his side, as though in pain. Yet his chief wife and a male attendant were covering him with a thick coat of black powder, and tying round his arms and legs a number of white scarfs, fastened in rosettes, with the long ends hanging down his sides. His head was turbaned in a scarlet handkerchief secured by a chaplet of small white cowries; and he wore armlets of the same shells. On his neck was the ivory necklace, formed in long curved points. To complete his royal attire according to Fijian idea, he had on a very large new *masi*, the train being wrapped in a number of loose folds at his feet.

"The conflicting emotions which passed through my mind at that moment cannot be described. I had gone there to beg that the old man might be buried alone; but he was not dead. I had hoped to have prevented murder; but two victims lay dead at my feet. I came to the young king to ask for the life of women; but it now seemed my duty to demand that of his father. Yet, should my plea be successful, it would cause other murders on a future day. Perplexed in thought, with a deep gloom on my mind, feeling my blood curdle and 'the hair of my flesh stand up,' I approached the young king, whom I could only regard with abhorrence. He seemed greatly moved, put his arm round and embraced me, saying, before I could speak, 'See! the father of us two is dead.' 'Dead!' I exclaimed, in a tone of surprise: 'dead! No.' 'Yes,' he answered: 'his spirit is gone. You see his body move; but that it does unconsciously.' Knowing that it would be useless to dispute the point, I ceased to care for the father, and went on to say that the chief object of myself and my colleague was to beg him to 'love us, and prevent any more women from being strangled, as he could not by multiplying the dead render any benefit to his father.' He replied, 'There are only two; but they shall suffice. Were not you missionaries here, we would make an end of all the women sitting around.'

"Preparations being made for removing the bodies, we, having no further cause for staying, retired from 'the large house.' In doing so, I noticed an interesting female, oiled and dressed in a new *liku*, carrying a long bamboo, the top of which contained about a pint of water, which, as the bodies were carried out at one door, she poured on the threshold of another, and then retired by the way she came. The words of the widow of Tekoah were thus brought, with peculiar force, to my mind:—'For we must needs die, and are as water spilt on the ground, which cannot be gathered up again.' My inquiry into the origin and meaning of this act resulted in nothing satisfactory. Neither could I learn why the side of the house was broken down to make a passage for the aged king to be carried through, when there were sufficient doorways close at hand. The bodies of the strangled women, having been secured in mats, were carried on biers to the sea-side. They were placed one on either end of a canoe, with the old king on the front deck, attended by the queen and the mata, who with a fan kept the insects off him. Thus was Tuithakau carried to Weilangi, to the sepulchre of the kings.

"Tongans were appointed to bury the king. The grave had been dug by the people of the place, and lined with mats, on which the Tongans laid the bodies of the women, and on them the once powerful chief. The shell ornaments were taken off his person, which was then covered with cloth and mats, and the earth heaped upon him. He was heard to cough after a considerable quantity of soil had been thrown in the grave. These latter particulars I received from those who buried him, as I could not by my presence seem to sanction the unnatural deed."

These people sometimes live to an old age, and when the hour of death is allowed to approach naturally, and the dying one is respectable, or the head of a family, the scene is certainly affecting. The patriarch calls his children around him, that he may say farewell and give his parting advice. This is generally commenced in the same way:—"I am going. You will remain."

At that hour of death, he never forgets an enemy, and at that time he never forgives one. The dying man mentions his foe, that his children may perpetuate his hatred—it may be against his own son—and kill him at the first opportunity. The name of the hated one is uttered aloud, if not as the object of immediate vengeance, yet of gloomy and disastrous predictions, which never fail to reach the ears where they are least welcome. The impression made on the minds of those to whom the carrying out of their dark purport is intrusted is indelible. Thus, with the deep marks of a murderous, unforgiving spirit upon him, does the heathen pass away to his account. At some funerals priests attend, and superintend the ceremonies. A grave, rarely more than three feet deep, is prepared. When the rites are finished, mats are laid at the bottom, and the body or bodies, wrapped in other mats and native cloth, are placed thereon, the edges of the under mats folding over all. The earth is then thrown in. Many yards of the man's *masi* are often left out of the grave, and carried in festoons over the branches of a neighboring tree.

Over some of the graves a small roof is built, three or six feet high, the gables of which are filled in with sinnet. Common graves are only edged with stones, or have nothing more than one set at the head and another at the foot.

One pretty custom is observed at Lakemba. A procession of women go forth, each bearing a basket of pure white sand, with which to cover the grave,—one part, in a clear, musical tone, singing, "*E-ui-e*," while the rest respond, "*E-yara*." Yet this was ascertained to be mere ceremony, with no appropriate feeling, when loud laughter from the women greeted the ear.

So strong is the desire for a friend to have company in the spirit-land, that even the Christians, who now disbelieve their former traditions, could not conceal their joy when they found that, one of their chiefs having been killed, a ball at the same time entered the body of a young man. It seemed to them a pleasant thought that he would not be alone.

But the heathen not only desires his friend to have companions, but he sends them after him. These victims are generally the wives of the deceased,—sometimes the mother; and if a chief has an intimate friend, it is deemed proper that he should die with him, in order to prevent any interruption of their intimacy. These victims are called "grass," and are laid in the grave first on mats, and their chief then placed over them.

It is seldom that a woman makes any objection to this sacrifice; for the fear of public opinion is stronger than that of death. Excited and urged on by her friends and relations, who know that their neglect to kill their mother or sister will be construed into disrespect or indifference for the deceased,—knowing that if she refuses death her life will be insupportable from the privations and cruelties she will suffer,—she consents to die.

Some die courageously, others sullenly

or silently. They even have carried their mats in which they were to be wrapped, and then helped to dig their graves. They know but little of the future, and have but slight pleasure in the present.

A white man once rescued a woman, driving the murderers away. He took her home, and, after some pains, resuscitated her; but as soon as she became conscious, instead of thanking him for deliverance from death, she poured a torrent of abuse upon him, and ever after manifested the deepest hatred towards him.

When Mbati Namu was killed, the relatives of Sa Ndrungu, his chief wife, brought and offered her to his friends. A missionary presented his *soro* for her life; but it was neutralized by her friends presenting one to "press it down." He made another offering, gained his point, and sent the disappointed murderers about their business,—one holding a bottle of oil, another turmeric powder, and a third the instrument of death,—all sad at heart that these were not to be used. A short time after, in consequence of the dissatisfaction of her friends, the woman left the Christian village, crossed the river, and entered the house of the man who was most anxious to destroy her, taking her stand in the midst, so as to intimate that she gave herself up to his will. The missionary followed, and got permission from the dead chief's brother to take her back with him, and by taking his proffered hand she might have lived. She intimated her sense of his kind intention, but declined to accompany him. Next morning she was strangled.

Two women who were to be strangled together, and who knew something of the gospel, said to a teacher who had been trying to save their lives, "Our case is one to cause pity; but we *dare* not live: *our friends dare not save us!*"

But the greatest evils fall on the children, who are thus left, without father or mother, to the care of those who love their own children little and these orphans less. In one class of seventeen in the mission-school, nine were orphans. At a baptism on the

Vanua Levu, of nine boys three were brothers, and of the entire number but four of the parents were living, the rest having met violent deaths. This is but a glimpse of the appalling facts which an examination would develop. Surely the heart must be hard almost as that of the heathen that can coldly view these scenes and yet feel no desire to bless them with the good news the gospel brings.

CHAPTER VIII.

CANNIBALISM.

We come now to a subject almost too revolting to be dwelt upon; but, as "cannibalism among this people is one of their institutions, interwoven in the elements of society," it must be treated somewhat in detail.

Until recently, there were many who refused to believe in the existence of this horrible practice in modern times; but the evidence is too conclusive for any one now to doubt. The motives that actuate the cannibals are principally revenge and relish for human flesh. When they are talked to on the subject, the only answer both chiefs and common people have made is, that it is "good!"

Now, since they have discovered the extreme abhorrence in which Europeans hold the practice, they are very averse to speak of it.

There are few chiefs who are not foremost among their people in the indulgence of this horrible custom; yet some rare exceptions hate cannibalism, and never can be induced to taste human flesh.

They generally secure for this purpose the bodies of all slain in battle. Persons shipwrecked are considered to have been sent by the gods, and are never spared. A common, because easy, method of obtaining victims, is to seize the women who are fishing on the reefs. Women and some of the priests are forbidden to eat of the *bakolo;** but their abstinence is only public, for it is a well-known fact that women secretly partake of the food.

The following facts illustrate the reason of holding and the manner of supplying their feasts, and also show the heroism of two ladies belonging to the mission.

The Mbutoni tribe of Mbau are rovers,

---

* A human body for eating.

spending much of their time on the sea. In 1849, a large company of them returned to Mbau, after an absence of seven years, bringing an unusually large tribute to the king. Extraordinary exertions were made to entertain so large and profitable a company. As it was necessary to obtain human food for them, two youths were taken and killed. But this was not nearly enough. Ngavindi, the chief of the fishermen, and purveyor for the cannibal feasts, felt his personal honor involved in the matter. He was young, and was on intimate terms with the missionaries and had been much under their influence; but they were at this time absent from Mbau, and his fear of their disapprobation yielded to the dread of being disgraced by not entertaining his guests in a suitable manner. He called the people and priests together, and said to them, "We shall lose our renown. We shall not be dreaded or fed. We have provided no food for the visitors. We must go to it in earnest. We will seek for enemies to Mbau. If we cannot catch any enemies, we will kill some who are friendly; and, if we cannot get either friends or enemies, some of ourselves must be strangled. Otherwise, we shall be disgraced for not doing what is our special work. Others are procuring: we must have some human beings."

The priests promised success, and, covering the ends of their canoes with green leaves, they hid under some mangrove-bushes at one end of the adjacent islands.

Unconscious of their hidden foes and of the awful doom awaiting them, a company of women came down to the shore to catch shell-fish. As they were pursuing their occupation, the concealed cannibals rushed upon them: fourteen were taken, and one man who was with them was killed. The noise of the sacred drums announced to the people of Mbau the approach of the canoes with the victims, and eager crowds met them at the landing with loud rejoicings and congratulations.

The report of these deeds reached the mission-house at Viwa, a few miles distant, where Mrs. Lyth and Mrs. Calvert were alone with their children. The horrible tidings moved these Christian women most deeply; but what could they do? Their husbands were far away from them. To go among these savages, now maddened and excited by the prospect of the feast before them, and ask them to forego it and surrender the victims they had just secured, was surely a daring act for two Englishwomen to undertake. But this they determined to do; and, though in themselves they were weak, and the peril of death was before them, they went, trusting in "the Lord of hosts, their refuge and their strength." They knew that their husbands, had they been at home, would have dared all danger to save the victims from the sacrifice and the people from the sin. It was but right for them to do what they could to supply their place.

As they drew near Mbau, the fearful din grew louder. Yet above the firing of muskets, the roar of drums, and the shouts of the people, arose the agonizing cries of the victims. With horror the conviction pressed on them that they were too late! The murder had commenced!

Fear gave way to impatience at that wild warning, and the Englishwomen's voices urged the laboring boatmen to make better speed. They reached the beach, and were met by a *lotu* (Christian) chief, who dared to join them, saying, "Make haste! Some are dead; but some are alive!" Surrounded by an unseen guard which none might break through, the women of God passed through the blood-maddened cannibals unhurt. They pressed forward to the house of the old king Tanoa, the entrance to which was strictly forbidden to all women.

It was no time for ceremony now. With a whale's tooth in each hand, and still accompanied by the Christian chief, they thrust themselves into the grim presence of the king, and prayed their prayer of mercy. The old man was startled at the audacity of the intruders. His hearing was dull, and they raised their voices higher to plead for their dark sisters' lives. The king said, "Those who are dead are dead; but those who are still alive shall live only." At that word, a man ran to Ngavindi, to stop his butchery, and returned to say that five still lived; the rest of the fourteen were killed. But the messengers of pity could not leave their work unfinished. They went to the house of the murderer, and found him sitting in state, in full dress, but evidently very uncomfortable. He winced under the sharp rebuke of the missionaries' wives, and muttered something about his friendliness to the *lotu* (Christianity). Even in cannibal Mbau, all did not consent to the deed of darkness. Thakombau's chief wife and Ngavindi's wife had already secured the life and liberty of two of the victims; and when Mrs. Calvert and Mrs. Lyth left there were others who blessed them for their work of love.

Disgusting as is this subject, a book on Fiji would be defective were it passed by in silence. Yet we will but slightly lift the veil to show the depths of degradation to which depraved man can fall when left to himself.

"Cannibalism," says Mr. Williams, "does not confine its selection to one sex or a particular age. I have seen the gray-headed and children of both sexes devoted to the oven. I have labored to make the murderers of females ashamed of themselves, and have heard their cowardly cruelty defended by the assertion that such victims were doubly good,—because they ate well, and because of the distress it caused their husbands and friends."

"Native warriors carry their revenge beyond death: so that bodies slain in battle are often mutilated in a frightful manner,—a treatment which is considered neither mean nor brutal. When the bodies of enemies are procured for the oven, the event is published by a peculiar beating of the drum, which alarmed me even before I was informed of its import. Soon after hearing it, I saw two canoes steering for the island, while some one on board struck the water, at intervals, with a long pole, to denote that they had killed some one. When sufficiently near, they began their fiendish war-dance, which was answered by the indecent dance of the women. On the boxed end of one of the canoes was a human corpse, which was cut adrift and tumbled into the water soon after the canoe touched land, when it was tossed to and fro by the rising and falling waves until the men had reported their exploit, when it was dragged ashore by a vine tied to the left hand. A crowd, chiefly females, surrounded the dead man, who was above the ordinary size, and expressed most unfeelingly their surprise and delight. 'A man, truly! a ship! a land!' The warriors, having rested, put a vine round the other wrist of the *bakolo*,—dead body designed for eating,—and two of them dragged it, face downwards, to the town, the rest going before and performing the war-dance, which consists in jumping, brandishing of weapons, and two or three, in advance of the main body, running towards the town, throwing their clubs aloft, or firing muskets, while they assure those within of their capability to defend them. A song was uttered in a wild monotone, finished with shrill yells.

"On reaching the middle of the town, the body was thrown down before the chief, who directed the priest to offer it in due form to the war-god. Fire had been placed in the great oven, and the smoke rose above the old temple, as the body was again drawn to the shore to be cut up. The carver used a piece of slit bamboo, with which, after having washed the body in the sea, he cut off the several members, joint by joint. The several parts were then folded in leaves and placed in the oven.

"Revenge is undoubtedly the main cause of cannibalism in Fiji, but by no means invariably so. I have known many cases in which such a motive could not have been present. Sometimes, however, this principle is horribly manifested.

"A woman taken from a town besieged by Ra Undreunde,* and where one of his

---

* A most noted cannibal, who was said to have eaten nine hundred persons.

friends had been killed, was placed in a large wooden dish and cut up alive, that none of the blood might be lost. In 1850, Tuikilakila inflicted a severe blow on his old enemies the Natewans, when nearly one hundred of them were slain, among whom was found the body of Ratu Rakesa, the king's own cousin. The chiefs of the victorious side endeavored to obtain permission to bury him, since he held the high rank of Rakesa, and because there was such a great abundance of *bakolo*. 'Bring him here,' said Tuikilakila, 'that I may see him.' He looked on the corpse with unfeigned delight. 'This,' said he, 'is a most fitting offering to Na Tavasara (the war-god). Present it to him: let it then be cooked, and reserved for my own consumption. None shall share with me. Had I fallen into his hands, he would have eaten me: now that he has fallen into my hands, I will eat him.' And it is said that he fulfilled his word in a few days, the body being lightly baked at first, and then preserved by repeated cooking."

"When I first knew Loti, he was living

at Na Ruwai. A few years before, he killed his only wife and ate her. She accompanied him to plant taro, and, when the work was done, he sent her to fetch wood, with which he made a fire, while she, at his bidding, collected leaves and grass to line the oven, and procured a bamboo to cut up what was to be cooked. When she had cheerfully obeyed his commands, the monster seized his wife, deliberately dismembered her, and cooked and ate her, calling some to help him in consuming the unnatural feast. The woman was his equal, one with whom he lived comfortably; he had no quarrel with her or cause of complaint. Twice he might have defended his conduct to me, had he been so disposed, but he only assented to the truth of what I here record. The only motives could have been a fondness for human flesh, and a hope that he should be spoken of and pointed out as a terrific fellow."

But let this suffice. The horrible facts of the cannibalism of the Fijians must be brought to light. We will not detail them further.

This custom makes the position of the missionaries among them peculiarly trying. Well may Captain Wilkes, in speaking of the gentleness and refinement of the missionary ladies, wonder how they can endure such a life. They could not, were they not sustained by a strength above their own. "God is their help and their shield, because they trust in his holy name." For him, and for the precious immortal souls of those whom Satan has bound in chains of sin, they leave home and kindred to dwell amid unspeakable horrors. They follow Christ; and he will be their everlasting reward.

Fijian Clubs.

CHAPTER IX.

WAR IN FIJI.

Fiji is rarely free from war and its attendant evils. When on his feet, the Fijian is always armed; when working in his garden, or lying on his mat, his arms are always at hand. This, however, is not to be attributed to his bold or choleric temper, but to suspicion and dread. Fear arms the Fijian. His own heart tells him that no one could trust him and be safe, whence he infers that his own security consists in universal mistrust of others. The club or spear is the companion of all his walks; but it is only for defence. This is proved by every man you meet: in the distance you see him with his weapon shouldered; getting nearer, he lowers it to his knee, gives you the path, and passes on. This is invariable, except when the people meet purposely to fight, or when two enemies come unexpectedly together. When war is decided upon between two powers, a formal message to that effect is interchanged, and informal messages in abundance, warning each other to strengthen their fences and carry them up to the sky. Councils are held, in which future action is planned. Before going to war with men, they study to be right with the gods. Ruined temples are rebuilt, some half buried in weeds are brought to light, and new ones erected. Costly offerings are brought to the gods, and prayers presented for the utter destruction of the enemy. Much confidence is placed in the god's help thus purchased. When it was said to a small party on their way to war, " You are few," they promptly replied, " Our allies are the gods."

Yet their dependence on their gods is not so entire as to make them indifferent to human assistance. If the tribe be a powerful one, it probably has under its protection smaller tribes, who are expected to assist their ally in time of war. They know very well that a refusal to give their aid would be disastrous to them. Sometimes an appeal is made to a friendly neighbor: a favorable answer is returned by sending a club or spear, and the message, "I have sent my club: by-and-by I will follow."

Visitors are always expected to assist the chief who entertains them.

The declaration of war having been made, both parties earnestly prepare for battle. As there is no regular army, the forces are collected in various ways: the only qualification required of a warrior is ability to handle some sort of weapon.

It is not often that a force of more than a thousand is raised. The army is collected by the *taqa*, a kind of review held at each town on the line of march. First comes the leader, and then others, singly at the beginning, but afterwards in companies of six, or ten, or twenty. It is impossible to tell all that is said when many are speaking at once; but there is no lack of bragging, if single challengers may be taken as specimens. One man runs up to the chief, brandishes his club, and exclaims, "Sir, do you know me? Your enemies soon will!" Another, darting forward, says, "See this hatchet, how clean! To-morrow it will be bathed in blood!" One cries out, "This is my club, the club that never yet was false!" The next, "This army moves to-morrow; then you shall eat dead men till you are surfeited!" A man, striking the ground violently with his club, boasts, "I cause the earth to tremble: it is I who meet the enemy to-morrow!" "See," exclaims another, "I hold a musket and a battle-axe! If the musket miss fire, the hatchet will not!" On one occasion a young man stepped towards a king, holding a pole used as an anchor, and said, "See, sire, the anchor of Natewa!* I will do thus with it!" And he broke the pole across his knee. A man, swinging a ponderous club, said, "This club is a defence, a shade from the heat of the sun, and the cold of the rain." Glancing at the chief, he added, "You may come under it." A fiery youth ran up, as though

---

* The place against which they were going to fight.

breathless, crying out, "I long to be gone! I am impatient!" One of the same kind said, "Ah, ah! these boasters are deceivers! I only am a true man: in the battle you shall find me so." These "great swelling words" are listened to with mingled laughter and applause. The fighting-men have their bodies covered with black powder; some, however, confine this to the upper part only. An athletic warrior thus powdered, so as to make his skin wear a velvet-like blackness, has a truly formidable appearance, his eyes and teeth gleaming with very effective whiteness. If the chief intends attacking a fortress, the difficulties in his way are often great, as the mountains afford many and safe fastnesses, of which the weaker tribes generally avail themselves, often fortifying them with much skill.

The fortress of Nateva Matua is an immense rock, not unlike an old feudal castle in appearance. It is perpendicular on every side but one, where a path only wide enough for one person winds precipitously downward. The top of the mountain is flat, and

victory with exaggerated boastings. Yet so frequent are their conflicts that the annual loss of life from this cause has been estimated at fifteen hundred or two thousand, without including the widows strangled in consequence.

The introduction of fire-arms, increasing the danger, has diminished the amount of war. Formerly the chiefs were held in such reverence that they were rarely harmed in battle; but now the bullet proves so often fatal to them that their relish for war has decreased.

The natives are said to be so expert that they can see the flash of a gun and fall on the ground in time to let the bullet pass over them.

In treating for peace, the common method is to send a messenger with a whale's tooth as a token of submission. The conditions made by the conquerors are often severe. The conquered tribe is frequently required to give up the "right of soil," which is done by sending the victorious party a basket containing soil from their land; after this they are expected to render annual tribute. Sometimes they are obliged to crawl on their hands and knees to their conquerors, and, with their heads in the dust, to beg for pardon and mercy. When peace is concluded, both parties throw down their arms.

But submission often does not avail to stem the tide of cruelty that overwhelms the defeated party. The barbarities used towards captives and the bodies of those slain would be incredible, had they not been witnessed.

Treachery in war, as in ordinary life, is of frequent occurrence.

The horrors perpetrated in sacking a town are truly awful. Instances have been known of people, singly and in companies, committing suicide rather than be subject to the outrages of their conquerors.

It is customary throughout Fiji to give honorary names to such as have clubbed a human being of any age or either sex during a war. The new epithet is given with the complimentary prefix *Koroi*. I once asked a man why he was called Koroi.

"Because," he replied, "I, with several other men, found some women and children in a cave, drew them out and clubbed them, and then was *consecrated*." If the man killed has been of distinguished rank, the slayer is allowed to take his name; or he is honored by being styled the *comb*, the *dog*, the *canoe*, or the *fort* of some great living chief. Warriors of rank receive proud titles; such as "the divider of" a district, "the waster of" a coast, "the depopulator of" an island,—the name of the place in question being affixed.

Defensive armor is rarely worn by the Fijian warrior. His skin is oiled and covered with a bluish-black powder, his face painted, and his hair dressed, and even to foreign eyes he presents a fine appearance. His tall figure exhibits strength and manliness; his martial carriage, his proud step, and his eyes gleaming with restlessness and excitement, make it difficult to believe that he can ever be a coward. Chiefs there are whose brave appearance is a true index to their character. The arms chiefly in use are clubs, spears, slings, battle-axes, bows and arrows, and muskets. Of these the two first are the favorite weapons. The spears are often ten or fifteen feet long, and are used with fatal effect. Some are barbed, others armed with the thorns of the sting-ray, while others still are made of a wood which bursts when moist, so as to be very difficult to extract from a wound.

These weapons all have significant names, such as "damaging beyond hope," or, with more subtle meaning, "the priest is too late."

In a siege arrows are used with effect, and the bow—in itself a poor weapon, as made by them—is handled with much skill by the women.

The instances are rare where there is aught to excite admiration in the character of the Fijian warrior. The jealous pride of the chiefs, and the existence of so many independent governments in such close proximity, with suspicious distrust of each other common to all, sufficiently account for the constant presence of war among them. The love of glory or genuine patriotism seldom leads them into battle. They are sometimes heroic in words, but the dangers and privations of war generally find them timid and effeminate. Their estimate of life is so low that they are often careless in throwing it away; but it is seldom that a noble emotion or principle influences them to self-sacrifice.

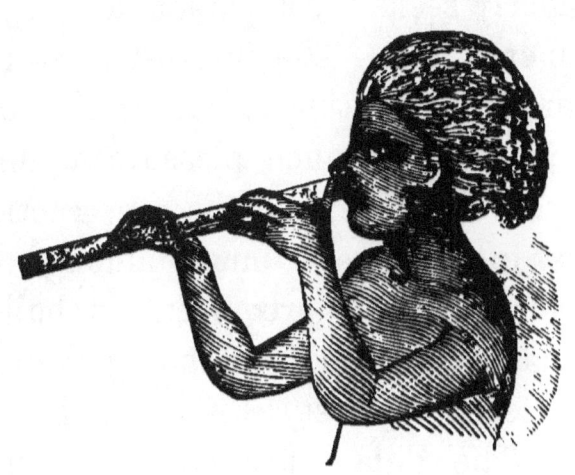

THE NOSE FLUTE.

CHAPTER X.

SOCIAL HABITS.

Notwithstanding the many disadvantages under which the Fijian lives, he is not without the enjoyments of social life. He eagerly seeks a companion, and delights in a merry jest. The interest shown in a tale, and the shouting in chorus of a native song, prove how much pleasure he finds in society. The form and the construction of houses in Fiji vary much among different tribes. The improvement in building-tools has made a corresponding change for the better in their style of building in late years. The Fijians are said, by an intelligent visitor among them, to have made considerable progress in architecture; and he adds that they are the only people he has seen, called by Europeans "savages," who manifest a taste for the fine arts.

Where part of the floor of a house is raised, forming a dais, which by day is the divan and by night the bed of a chief, it is covered with mats, varying in number from two to ten, and spread over a thick layer of dried grass and elastic ferns, while on them are placed two or three neat wooden or bamboo pillows. Over this hangs the mosquito-curtain, which is generally large enough to hang across the house, thus giving to one end of it an air of comfort. Checkered baskets, gourds, and bottles for scented oil are hung about the walls; and in a conspicuous place stands or hangs the yaqona bowl, with a strainer and cup. In various parts are suspended fans, a sunshade made of the leaf of the cabbage-palm, an oil-dish of dark wood, and several food-dishes of wood or wicker-work. On a slight frame behind the curtain stands a chest or two, with a musket hanging above, and perhaps an axe and spade beneath. Along the foot of the wall rest oblong wooden bowls with four feet, or round earthen pans with none. If there is any arrow-root, it is preserved in coarse, wide-mouthed jars; and one or more glazed water-vessels have a place near the hearth or bed, set in a nest of dry grass. The other domestic apparatus is found near the hearth, and comprises nets, a bone knife for cutting bread from the pit, and another of foreign make for cutting up yams, &c.; a concave board, four or six feet long, on which to work up the bread, and round stones for mashing the same; coarse baskets for vegetables, cocoa-nut and bamboo vessels for salt and fresh water, and soup-dishes, and a ladle made of the nut-shell. On the hearth, each set on three stones, are several pots, capable of holding from a quart to five gallons. Near these are a cord for binding fuel, a skewer for trying cooked food, and, in the better houses, a wooden fork,—a luxury which probably the Fijian enjoyed when our worthy ancestors were wont to take hot food in their practised fingers.

The facilities for boiling food and making hot drinks form one of the advantages almost peculiar to the Fijian as contrasted with the other islanders. The Fijians also have the

SOCIAL HABITS.

distinction of using mosquito-curtains, of separate sleeping-rooms for the young men, and a better style of houses.

The natives usually take two meals in the day; the principal one being in the afternoon or evening. Their general food is light and plain, fish being highly esteemed. Contrary to the taste of civilized gourmands, these people will have all their meat quite fresh, and some small kinds of fish are eaten alive as a relish. They have also dishes from shell-fish, soups, various kinds of bread, and teas made from grasses and leaves.

The refreshing milk of the cocoa-nut is much used by the Fijian; but his general beverage is water. In drinking without a cup, the head is thrown back with the mouth opened, the water-vessel held several inches above the lips, and a stream allowed to run down the throat,—a process whereby a novice is more likely to be choked than refreshed. This method of drinking is adopted to avoid touching the vessel with their lips, a practice to which they strongly object. To drink from the long bamboos sometimes used is no easy task. These vessels are from two to ten feet long. One of the longest will hold two gallons; and to slake one's thirst from its open end, while a native gradually elevates the other, requires care, or a cold bath will be the unsought result.

The meal of a chief only differs from that of a common man in that the food is of better quality, more frequently served, and received with greater form. If the chief is not *tabu* as to the hands, he may feed himself or not, as he chooses; but if *liga tabu*, he must be fed by another, generally his chief wife. While he is eating, everybody present retains a sitting position,—the attitude of respect; when he has done, he pushes the dish a little way from him, and each person claps his hands several times. Water is next brought to the chief, who washes his hands and rinses his mouth, after which, in some parts, hands are again clapped by every one in the house.

A favorite Fijian drink is the *ava*, or *yaqona*, a narcotic and stupefying liquor, extracted from a root. On the island of

Somo-somo, early in the morning the king's herald stands in front of the royal abode, and shouts, at the top of his voice, "Yaqona!" Hereupon, all within hearing respond, in a sort of scream, "*Mama!*"—"Chew it!" At this signal the chiefs, priests, and leading men gather round the well-known bowl, and talk over public affairs, or state the work assigned for the day, while their favorite draught is being prepared. When the young men have finished the chewing, each deposits his portion, in the form of a round dry ball, in the bowl, the inside of which thus becomes studded over with a large number of these separate little masses. The man who has to make the grog takes the bowl by the edge and tilts it towards the king, or, in his absence, to the chief appointed to preside. A herald calls the king's attention to the slanting bowl, saying, "Sir, with respects, the yaqona is collected." If the king thinks it enough, he replies, in a low tone, "*Loba,*" "Wring it;" an order which the herald communicates to the man at the bowl in a louder voice. The water is then called for, and gradually poured in, a little at first, and then more, until the bowl is full, or the master of the ceremonies says, "Stop!" the operator in the mean time gathering up and compressing the chewed root. Then follows the "*science* of the process," which consists of the final rolling, twisting, and compression of the root, and straining of the liquid until it is clear and ready for drinking. This preparation of the *yaqona* is of great interest to the people, hundreds of whom sometimes closely watch the operator, who develops much skill and graceful action.

The customs observed differ on the various islands in some particulars, but are similar in general character.

Very few Fijians drink to excess. The intemperate are easily distinguished by their inflamed eyes and a scaly appearance of the skin. By one or two ordinary draughts a stupor is produced, from which the drinker manifests an unwillingness to be aroused.

The Fijians hold feasts, for which, when on a large scale, preparations commence months beforehand. Yams and taro are planted with special reference to it, a *tabu* is put upon pigs and nuts, and the turtle-fishers are sent to set their nets. As the time approaches, messengers are sent far and near to announce the day appointed. This announcement, which is a respectful way of inviting the guests, is made to the several chiefs, and through them to their people. The invitations are liberal, including all the male population of the town or district to which the Mata is sent.

On the part of the entertainers there is a vigorous effort at display. A day or two beforehand, every one is full of activity,—the king issuing orders, the Matas communicating them to the people, and the people carrying them out. The ovens are prepared during the previous night, when the chopping of fuel and squealing of pigs is heard in every direction, while the flames from the ovens yield a light greatly helping the labors of the cooks. The baking of all kinds of food, and the making of all kinds of puddings, are intrusted to the men. The ovens, which are holes or pits sunk in the ground, are sometimes eight or ten feet deep and fifty feet in circumference; and in one of these several pigs and turtles and a large quantity of vegetables can be cooked. English roasters of an entire ox or sheep might learn some useful philosophy from the Fijian cook, whose method insures the thorough and equal baking of the whole carcass. The oven is filled with firewood, on which large stones are placed, and the fire introduced. As soon as the fuel is burnt out, the food is placed on the hot stones, some of which are put inside the animals to be cooked whole. A thick coat of leaves is now rapidly spread over all, and on these a layer of earth about four inches thick. When the steam penetrates this covering, it is time to remove the food; whereupon the lull that followed the closing of the oven gives place to renewed activity, as the men, besides having rested, have also regaled themselves on the hearts, livers, kidneys, &c. of the pigs they have killed, and which tit-bits they ate *ex officio*. Thus refreshed, they proceed to plait green baskets, beat up the taro paste with ponderous pestles, prepare the large, beautiful leaves to receive the paste and sauce, tie them up, count, report, and carry them away with as much alacrity as though they had lost sight of the characteristic counsel of their forefathers, to "go gently, that they may live long."

On these occasions profusion is always aimed at: waste is the consequence, and want follows. At one public feast a missionary saw two hundred men employed nearly six hours in collecting and piling cooked food. There were six mounds of yams, taro, *vakalolo*, pigs, and turtles: these contained about fifty tons of cooked yams and taro, fifteen tons of sweet pudding, seventy turtles, five cart-loads of yaqona, and about two hundred tons of uncooked yams. One pudding at a Lakemba feast measured twenty-one feet in circumference.

The head-men of the visitors sit to receive the food, as it is brought and piled before them, expressing their approval by saying, aloud, "*Vinaka! Vinaka!*" "Good! Good!" The duty of distributing the food, on account of the extreme punctiliousness of the people about rank, is attended with considerable difficulty. A chief is honored or slighted according to the quantity or quality of the food set before him; and nothing of this kind can escape notice, as every eye eagerly watches the proceedings. When there are several chiefs in the party, an accurate knowledge of the grade of each is necessary to avoid error. The food having been divided into as many portions as there are tribes, the Tui-rara, beginning with the first in rank, shouts out, "The share of Lakemba!" or whichever may take preference. If a foreigner should be observed among the spectators, he is sure not to be passed by, but a portion—very likely enough for twenty men—will be given to him. When each tribe has received its share, a redivision takes place, answering to the number of its towns; these, again, subdivide it among the head families, who, in their turn, share what they get with their dependants, and these with the individual members of their household, until no one is left without a portion, the food disappearing forthwith, with a rapidity which baffles calculation. The males eat in the open air, sending the women's share to their houses. Should some wayfarer pass by, he is pressingly invited to partake of the entertainment, and allowed to dip in the same dish with those who bid him.

Indeed, while witnessing such a scene, it is only by an effort of the mind that one can believe that a people so blithe and benevolent are capable of the atrocities with which they are charged. But beneath all that apparent pleasantness and repose there lurk strong elements of disquiet. A misarrangement or impropriety would cause a hundred bright eyes to flash with anger, which, though suppressed then, would burst forth with a deadlier effect on a future day.

Among the Fijians the rules of politeness are minute and receive scrupulous attention. They affect the language, and are seen in forms of salutation, in attention to strangers at meals, and in dress. In saluting a chief, a shout of reverence, called the *tama*, is used, except in a few cases. Equals, on meeting each other early in the day, say, "*Sa yadra*," "Awake," or, "You are awake;" in the evening, "*Sa moce*," or, "*Lá ki moce*," "Sleep," or, "Go to sleep."

On a visit of a person from a distance, as soon as he is seated, the master of the house gently claps his hands three or four times, and says, very much in Eastern style, "Come with peace!" The name of the place whence the visitor has come is generally added, or the name of the house, should he reside in the same town. Thus, the wife of the king of Somo-somo would be welcomed with, "Come with peace, the lady from Nasima." The parting kiss of the Fijians is peculiar, one *smelling* the other with a strong sniff. Equals do this on each other's faces. A chief of lower grade will thus salute a superior's hand, and inferiors will embrace the knees and smell the feet of a chief. Shaking hands has been introduced by the missionaries, and is in high repute. "*Sa loloma*," "My love to you," owes its origin

SOCIAL HABITS. 139

to the same source, and is used by all the Christians.

The existence of expressions equivalent to our "Mr.," "Sir," and "Madam" does much towards polishing the intercourse of this people; and it is remarkable that they only of the island groups in the South Seas have these terms in regular use.

Sleep and tobacco are among the leading comforts of the Fijian. He follows activity with slumber from which he hates to be aroused. Tobacco, though known only for about thirty years, is in such high favor that its use is all-but universal, children as well as adults indulging in it freely. The native method of smoking is decidedly social. A small cigarette, formed by folding leaf-tobacco in a strip of dead banana-leaf, is lit, and passed to four or six persons in succession. Having to swim across a river does not interrupt this transfer; for the same cigar may be conveyed from one bank to the other in several different mouths.

Sports of different kinds occupy many of the leisure hours of the people. A favorite one among the girls consists in keeping eight oranges in the air above the head at one time. Games closely resembling "hide-and-seek," "blind-man's buff," and "hop, skip, and jump," as played by American children, are common among these dark Fijian youths.

Some of the games played by the boys are of a cruel character. One of the chiefs told an Englishwoman that one of his favorite games, when a boy, was to fix a sharply-pointed stick in the ground, and then jump in such a way that the companion whom he had dared to follow him would run it in his foot. It is not strange that boys accustomed to such pastimes should not shrink from cruelty when they grow to manhood.

A swing, consisting of a single rope or strong vine, with a loop at the end in which to insert the foot, is fastened to a tree. The swinger is then pushed off, and away he goes as far as his rope of thirty or fifty feet will send him.

Men and women wrestle on top of a hill: if either is thrown, they roll down together, much to the delight of the spectators, and occasional mortification of one who may be hurt.

Several amusements belong to the water, such as chasing each other, wrestling, and diving. Shoals of men or of women are seen, on a calm day, striking away from the shore with gleeful notes, or that hearty abandonment of broad-mouthed mirth for which they are so famous. In the game of *ririka*, an upright post is fixed at the edge of a reef, and the upper end of a long cocoa-nut-tree rested on it, so as to form an easy ascent, with the point projecting beyond the post and raised about fifteen or twenty feet above the surface of the water. The natives run up this incline in a continuous single file, and their rapidly succeeding plunges keep the water all round white with foam. Youngsters use the surf-boards which are so often found in Polynesia.

Canoe-racing is also a favorite Fijian amusement. They are fond of their rude and monotonous music, but seem to be insensible to the harmony of flutes and melodious instruments.

Their musical instruments are the conch-shell, which is blown, pandean pipes, in which reeds of different lengths are ranged together, jews'-harps, made of bamboo strips, and the nose-flute, played by air from the nostril. They have also drums, large and small, made of a log hollowed like a trough, with cross-pieces near the ends. The long stick, in the illustration, is that used in the dance.

But the chief amusement of the people is the dance. The king of Levuka had a grand "club dance" for Captain Wilkes's entertainment; and the description of one serves for most of this class of their performances. For several days beforehand great preparations were made, and all the chiefs and people subject to this king were called to assist. On the appointed day the visitors were escorted to the *bure,* or temple, and placed on the platform, having a clear view of the square in front. This was enclosed by a stone wall, and filled with numerous spectators. About a hundred boys and men— the musicians—sat on one side, while an open

Musical Instruments.

Page 142.

space was left in the centre for the dancers. Suddenly shouts of laughter greeted the waiting assembly, as a clown appeared dressed in vines and leaves, with only his hands and feet uncovered. He wore a large mask like a bear's head, painted black on one side and orange on the other. He carried two clubs, a long and a short one; and his grotesque movements were greeted with loud applause. The musicians struck up a monotonous tune, singing and playing in excellent time. The dancers, in gala dress, and about a hundred in number, now issued, two by two, from behind a large rock. Around their white turbans the chiefs wore tasteful wreaths of flowers and leaves. The motions of the dancers were at first slow and measured, the principal action consisting in changing the position of their clubs. At the end of each strain of music they simultaneously advanced three steps, bowing gracefully to their visitors. When they had all entered the square, they became more violent *in* their movements, and went rapidly around, jumping and tramping heavily, while the clown comically mimicked the chiefs and prominent dancers.

When the dance was over, the performers piled their clubs before the visitors as a present. Captain Wilkes was not a little amused to see that many of them had substituted less valuable ones for those used in the dance. Of course they expected presents in return, which were given them.

The telling of stories, often of a very extravagant nature, is a favorite amusement with the Fijians. "Come, tell us a far-away tale," said a king to one of his attendants who had been to Australia. So he began and told him of guns he saw in Sydney, each of which took a keg of powder to prime; of a thousand saw-mills working in a river with no one near them, and making such a quantity of saw-dust that when he was four days' journey from them he was obliged to veil his eyes to keep it from blinding him. He wound up by saying "You talk about long houses in Fiji; but you should see the barracks where the soldiers in Sydney dwell. I was foolish enough to begin to fathom off with my arms, so as to measure it as we measure *tapa;* but after three months' fatigue I had to give it up as useless, because I could not see that I was any nearer the end than when I began."

This is a specimen of the tales with which they divert themselves for hours. Ventriloquists are common among them, and some few of the people possess skill in sleight-of-hand tricks.

The term *tabu, tapu, tambu,* or *taboo,* is familiar to the civilized world, and indicates precisely the same principle in every part of the South Seas. The force of the word can be fully realized only by a Polynesian. In Fiji it represents an institution despotic and merciless in operation, and to the enforcement of it the people yield without the slightest symptom of rebellion.

To *tabu* any thing is to effectually prevent its being touched or used until the *tabu* is removed. Nothing is too great or too small to be affected by it. Here it is seen tending a brood of chickens, and there it directs the energies of a kingdom. Its influence is wondrously diffused. Coasts, lands, rivers, and seas, animals, fish, fruit, and vegetables, houses, beds, pots, cups, and dishes, canoes, with all belonging to them and their management, dress, ornaments, and arms, things to eat and things to drink, the members of the body, manners and customs, language, names, temples, and even the gods also, all come under the influence of the *tabu*. It is put into operation by religious, political, or selfish motives; and idleness lounges for months beneath its sanction. Many are thus forbidden to raise or extend their hands in any useful employment for a long time. In this district it is *tabu* to build canoes; on that island it is *tabu* to erect good houses. When cocoa-nuts are to be tabued in any district, a mound of earth is thrown up by the road-side, a fence of reeds encircles it, and upon a post woven with the cocoa-nut tree leaf are hung cocoa-nuts covered with turmeric powder. This is illustrated in our engraving. Until the prohibition is removed, no nuts can be gathered in that district. Thus are men fettered

Cocoa-Nut Tabu.

Page 146.

and oppressed by heathenism in a thousand ways. The gospel brings not only hope for eternity, but liberty for this life.

The system is greatly favored by the chiefs, for by it they gain influence, supply their wants, and command at will their subjects.

A young boy once obtained leave from his father, the chief, to *tabu* all food then in the gardens, so that, while the prohibition lasted, no one could use even his own produce without first going to the young prince to ask permission. If any one dared to omit this ceremony, the prince, with his retinue of boys, was soon seen running towards the offender's house, carrying flags, blowing trumpets, &c. Each of the boys would snatch up any article he could lay his hands on, and then they all ran off again as swiftly and noisily as they came.

Persons who are afraid their property will be stolen endeavor to place it under a *tabu*.

In times of scarcity it is common to *tabu* certain articles to prevent famine by their injudicious use. The missionaries once felt the rigor of this act severely. Their supplies being delayed, and the pork and various other kinds of food *tabued*, they were subject for months to great inconvenience.

CHAPTER XI.

OCCUPATIONS.

THE Fijians have not the indolent habits common to most tropical nations. The Fijian is almost always busily employed: when not at war, he is boating, fishing, building, weaving nets, rolling sinnet, moulding earthen-ware, carving clubs and spears, planting, gathering, or in some way fully occupying his time.

The union of savage wildness with careful attention to agriculture is remarkable in the character of the Fijians; and it has been observed by visitors that they cultivate many kinds of produce unknown to the other Pacific islands.

Of yams (a root resembling the potato)

OCCUPATIONS.

there are in Fiji the usual varieties, and in some parts of the group two crops are raised in the year. Ordinary tubers of this valuable plant weigh from six to twelve pounds; extraordinary ones grow six or even nine feet long, and weigh from thirty to one hundred pounds. Sweet potatoes and sugarcane are also cultivated. But the chief staple among the Fijians is the *taro*, which forms the substitute for bread, and is much used in their cookery. The leaves and roots of the plant are eaten; and even the petiole, or foot-stalk, is used like our asparagus.

The *taro* root is oval in shape, and weighs from one to twelve pounds. It requires skilful cultivation; and the oblong *taro* beds terracing the hill-sides form a peculiar and beautiful feature in the scenery.

The well-known banana-tree is of great importance to the natives. There are in these islands thirty varieties of this tree, all differing in form and size of fruit. The bananas are used in a variety of modes of cooking, and of the young leaf water-proof covers for the head are made.

The *yaqona*, of which they make the *cava* or *ava*, their favorite narcotic drink, is an object of great attention in some parts of these islands.

The bread-fruit tree and the paper-mulberry are also of much importance, the latter supplying the natives with the principal material of their dress.

The preparation of the bark of this tree, and its manufacture into *masi* for clothing, forms the principal occupation of the women, and consists in the following process.

The bark is carefully stripped off in pieces as long as possible. Then it is steeped in water till it is pliable and the rough exterior can be removed by scraping with a shell. Two thicknesses together are then laid on a log, and so beaten with a wooden mallet that a breadth of two inches can be spread into a foot and a half. Several pieces are lapped together with *taro* starch or arrow-root till the cloth is sufficiently long, sometimes measuring a hundred or more yards. The width can be increased by joining in the same way. The artistic part of the manufacture is in the process of dyeing; and in this the women often exhibit much taste. The borders of mosquito-curtains are very elaborately ornamented, and are the especial pride of the Fijian lady. For these she uses a flat board, a black dye, and a pattern cut out of a banana-leaf. She places the pattern on the border, and with a pad of cloth steeped in the black dye she rubs the leaf over, and the dye remains in the figure upon the border.

The turban of the men is made of a fine preparation of the *masi*, beaten out till it is gauze-like in texture. The *liku*, or women's dress, is braided of the fibres of a wild root, grasses, or the bark of the *hibiscus*, beaten out and made into a broad variegated band. From this hangs a red or black fringe of from three to ten inches in depth.

Next in importance to the manufacture of cloth is that of mats. The number demanded of these articles is very great, as they are used for chairs, carpets, tables, sails, beds, and curtains. Wrapped in mats also the Fijians are buried.

"The wicker-work baskets of Fiji are strong, handsome, and useful beyond any I have seen at home or abroad," says the Rev. Mr. Lowry; and when we consider the perfection to which the English have brought the art of basket-making, this commendation of the Fijian work is certainly as high praise as he could well bestow.

The making of nets gives constant employment to many of these islanders. The process is the same as that employed for the same purpose in England. The nets used by the men are sometimes made of hibiscus, but generally of sinnet, which is the fibre of the cocoa-nut husk, well dried, combed, and braided. The natives roll it into balls, which are often very large. Mr. Williams mentions one that he measured, which was nine feet high and thirteen feet in circumference. The Fijians use sinnet for their best ropes, which are of various size and exceedingly strong.

The Fijian is also distinguished from all the South Sea islanders eastward in his potteries, where are produced various utensils

Fijian Pottery.

Page 153.

of red and brown ware. The drinking-vessels are often prettily designed, some being globular, some urn-shaped, others like three or four oranges joined together, the handle springing from each and meeting at the top; others, again, are made in the forms of canoes. Earthen arrow-root pans, dye-bowls, and fish-pots are in great demand. The greatest call, however, is for cooking-pots. Several of these are found in every house; and, as they are not very durable, the demand is brisk. The mode of manufacture is simple, and the articles are of good shape, well baked, and often glazed.

The dishes for the priests, oil-dishes, and yaqona-bowls, as well as the cannibal forks, are generally made of hard wood, often curiously formed, and ornamented with carving.

The weapons of Fijian war are many of them simple in their construction, while others evince much artistic skill in carving and inlaid work. The simple throwing clubs are furnished by the forest, and require but little handiwork to perfect them. Others are shaped on the tree while growing, and require constant superintendence till they are formed. A knotty mace is made by pulling up a young tree and cutting off the roots.

Their tools, until lately, were few and simple. The one principally used, with slight alterations to suit different purposes, was a hard stone ground to an edge and firmly tied to a wooden handle. Rats' teeth were used for fine carving, corals for files, and the pumice-stone for finishing off their work. Their first iron implements were procured from the Tongans, who had established commerce with Europeans some time before. The first knowledge they had of steel was from half of a ship-carpenter's draw-knife which had been broken off and ground down. This was highly prized and in great demand, and named Fulifuli, in honor of the chief who introduced it. Now, however, they are supplied from England and America with common tools; but the climate is injurious to more delicate instruments.

To illustrate the speed with which a Fijian builds his house, Mr. Williams says

Houses of Fiji.

Page 155.

that going out one morning he passed a company of carpenters who were just putting up the posts of a house. When he returned, an hour and a half later, he found the building nearly completed!

Ordinarily, to finish entirely a thatched house requires about ten days. A large house for a chief's dwelling, or a temple, is completed in two or three months. Some of their buildings are very handsome. A visitor, speaking of the dwelling of King Tanoa, of Mbau, says, "It surpasses in magnitude and grandeur any thing I have seen in these seas. It is one hundred and thirty feet long, forty-two feet wide, with massive columns in the centre, and strong, curious workmanship in every part."

The shape of the houses differs very much on the various islands. In one district, a village looks like an assemblage of square wicker baskets; in another, like so many rustic arbors; a third seems a collection of oblong hay-ricks, with holes in the sides; while in a fourth these ricks are conical.

Timber made from several different trees

is used for building-material, and grass, sugar-cane, or palm-leaves for thatching. The ridge-pole always projects beyond the eaves, and is ornamented with shells. The door-ways are so low that one is obliged to stoop in entering. In front of the entrance hangs a mat to serve as a door. The interior walls are ornamented with sinnet or grasses in different colors or patterns. A good artist in this work finds constant employment, and succeeds in producing a beautiful effect. The rooms are rarely partitioned; but at each end the floor is slightly elevated above the centre, to serve for sleeping-purposes, and is covered with soft mats and dotted with the little three-legged pillows. The fireplaces are in the centre of the room, and are exceedingly primitive in their construction, consisting of holes, surrounded by a hard curb of wood, and containing a few large stones, on which they build the fire and place the pots. A few fine houses have a shelf on which the pots are placed.

When a man wishes a house built, his application must be made to the proper officers, and the chief of the carpenters is then directed to build one according to his wishes. He employs as many men as he thinks proper.

A more animated scene than the thatching of a house in Fiji cannot be conceived. When a sufficient quantity of material has been collected round the house, the roof of which has been previously covered with a net-work of reeds, from forty to three hundred men and boys assemble, each being satisfied that he is expected to do some work, and each determined to be very noisy in doing it. The workers within pair with those outside, each tying what another lays on. When all have taken their places, and are getting warm, the calls for grass, rods, and lashings, and the answers, all coming from two or three hundred excited voices of all keys, intermixed with stamping down the thatch, and shrill cries of exultation from every quarter, make a miniature Babel, in which the Fijian—a notorious proficient in nearly every variety of halloo, whoop, and yell—fairly outdoes himself.

In putting down the posts of a house of any importance, it is common to bury a man with each one. He clasps it with his arms, and is supposed, in consideration of his sacrifice, to have power given him by the gods to hold it up.

The Fijian canoes were for a long time much better built than those of many of their neighbors.

A Tongan chief, visiting Fiji, was so convinced of the superiority of their canoes over those of his own people that he left his clumsy craft behind him and returned in one of Fijian build. When his people saw his new vessel, they abandoned their own style and built after the Fijian mould, and for more than a hundred years they have never deviated from the pattern then adopted.

These boats are generally double, the two parts united by a platform, which extends two or three feet beyond the sides of the canoes. The sail, made of pliable mats, fifteen or twenty feet long, appears out of all proportion to the rest of the vessel. The

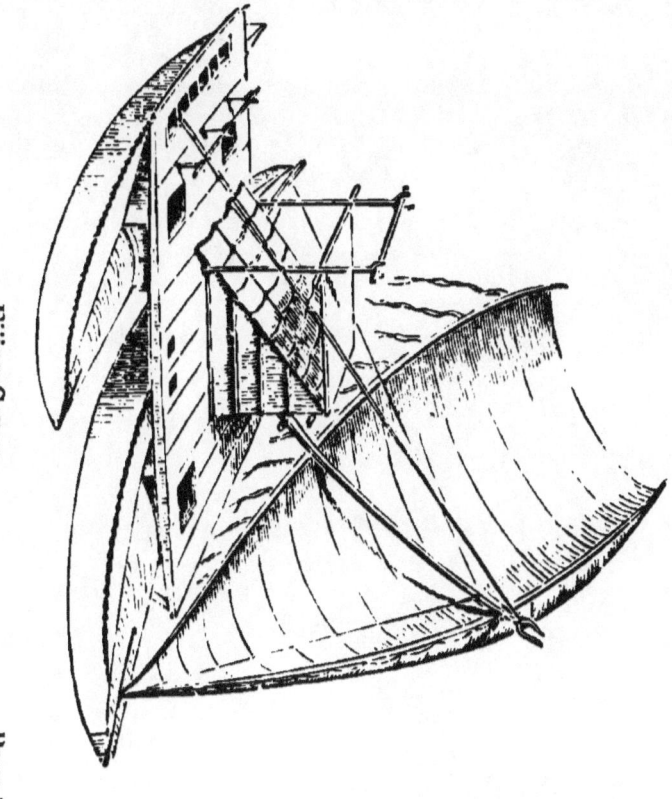

Fijian Canoe.

Page 150.

management of this is generally given to the chief; and it often requires care and skill to prevent the top-heavy craft from being upset. The ordinary vessels hold forty or fifty men, and are built, like the houses, by a contract with the chief of carpenters. Sailors are found on all the islands, but they especially abound in the Mbutoni and the Levuka tribes. They occupy a low rank in the community, but are skilful in nautical affairs, even the women possessing sufficient knowledge of them to perform the ordinary duties of seamen. The heathen sailor's life is a very merry one. The crew seem less like hirelings, with certain duties to perform, than like a gay party of pleasure-seekers. Jesting, laughing, singing, beating of drums, loud cries of thanks to favorable winds, and prayers to adverse ones, are continually heard; and thus they bound over the ocean, often turning from their prescribed route to fish or catch turtles, with entire forgetfulness of their main object.

This leads us to one of the Fijian's principal occupations,—viz., fishing. Turtle-fishing is an important and lucrative branch of this pursuit.

There are in the islands several different ways of catching turtles, all of them involving more or less danger. One of these is to attach floats to a large net of strong sinnet, and carry it on a canoe into deep water outside of the reef. The ends are brought back to the reef, making a semi-circular fence, which intercepts the turtle as he comes back from feeding. If he should turn and swim away from the net, he is frightened back by the loud shouting and stamping of the fishermen. After he is entangled, his capture is comparatively easy. In some methods of turtle-fishing the contest in the water with a strong and frantic fish is desperate, and the divers need all the agility and strength they possess to capture him.

The payment of the fishermen is regulated by their success. Turtle-fishers are generally attached to the household of a chief, acting under his orders, and rewarded by him.

Sometimes three or four turtles may be taken in a day; but from fifty to a hundred is thought good success for a season, which lasts from December to May. Of so much importance is this trade, that the white residents make strong efforts to monopolize it.

Biche-de-mar, or the sea-slug, a small fish caught on the reefs, is a valuable article of commerce, about thirty thousand dollars' worth being annually obtained, chiefly from Vanua Levu and Viti Levu. A chief and his men are generally employed by traders to obtain this fish.

Captain Wilkes speaks of a season's fishing while he was there, which yielded the trader twenty-five thousand pounds sterling, and had required a very small outlay. The fish have to be cured, for which purposes houses are built and constant labor expended.

The commerce of the Fiji Islands is not large. It began with Europeans about 1806, in an exchange of sandal-wood for various trifling articles. The supply of this wood has now almost entirely failed, the trees having nearly died out, and no pains being taken to renew them. Tortoise-shell and biche-de-mar are now the principal items of export trade, mostly carried on by Americans from Salem. The Fijian commerce consists mainly in barter, requiring a large supply of suitable goods in the hands of traders with them. Their chiefs are displeased with the payment of money, greatly preferring articles which are of immediate value to them, instead of useless foreign coin.

CHAPTER XII.

RELIGION.

A CONSPICUOUS building in every Fijian village is the *bure*, or temple. It is raised upon a foundation of from three to twenty feet above the ground. The ascent to it is by a plank, with steps cut on the upper side. The interior of the *bure* exhibits the highest skill of the Fijian in decoration and finish. Every timber is covered with the

Mbure of Na Tasavara.

Page 163.

most elaborate patterns in red and black sinnet, while the rafters, posts, walls, window-sashes, and door-frames are ornamented with the same material, which also hangs in heavy cords from the eaves. A variety of articles, such as hand-clubs, turbans, necklaces of flowers, &c., received as votive offerings, or by the priests as doctor's fees, adorn the room. A curtain of white *masi* hangs from the roof to the floor, and is the sacred path by which the god descends to inspire the priest.

In some of the temples small images are seen, used merely as ornaments, not as objects of worship; and at Mbau parts of the bodies of enemies are hung around the temple.

Although so much trouble and expense are given to building the *bure*, it is afterwards much neglected. Being rarely used for purposes of worship, it is principally occupied as a council-chamber and sleeping-place for distinguished persons in the village. When a king wishes to propitiate a god, he frequently repairs or erects a *bure*, but when the immediate occasion is past it falls into ruin again.

The priests possess great influence, although their power has for some time rapidly decreased. The only access the people have to their gods is through them; and, as the chiefs and priests are generally in league together, the decree of a god is pretty certain to be one that will suit the chiefs.

The rank of a priest is determined by that of his god. The office is mainly hereditary; but any man who has sufficient ability to inspire the people with a conviction of his power may become a successful priest.

"I knew a young man at Somo-somo," says Mr. Williams, "who paid dearly for a trick of this kind. He was hungry one day, and sat down a few paces from my garden-fence, and began to shake, priest-fashion, and call for bananas. Of course it was the god who wanted bananas, and bananas were immediately given him. This, you see, was an easier way of obtaining them than going to plant them.

"Well, he went on for some months, perhaps twelve, and fully established his reputation as a priest, and began to think himself somebody, and to wear a long train behind him, as the priests do.

"Tuikilakila, being annoyed at his assuming so much, and being, I suppose, rather doubtful as to the validity of his priesthood, sent for him one day to go to his house. He went, and Tuikilakila interrogated him after this manner:—'Who are you, that you should set up priest and make yourself somebody? I will kill you and eat you to-day; and if your god be a true god, he will eat me!' And he was as good as his word, too; for he lifted his ponderous club with his giant arm and clubbed him on the spot, put him in an oven, and baked and ate him. He had to eat him alone, as the people dared not eat a priest, as they feared the priest's god would inflict vengeance on them for it."

The priests usually form part of the personal retinue of the chiefs, and are provided for by them. When the supply of food does not satisfy them, however, they call the people together and declare to them a message from a god, upbraiding them for neglect to make offerings and threatening them with severe punishment. This terrifies the people to such a degree that they hasten to fill the priests' larder to overflowing. The priest always eats the substance of an offering, the god only requiring the *soul*.

One who intends to consult the oracle dresses and oils himself, and, accompanied by a few others, goes to the priest, who, we will suppose, has been previously informed of the intended visit, and is lying near the sacred corner, getting ready his response. When the party enters, he rises, and sits so that his back is near to the white cloth by which the god visits him, while the others occupy the opposite side of the *bure*. The principal person presents a whale's tooth, states the purport of the visit, and expresses a hope that the god will regard him with favor. Sometimes there is placed before the priest a dish of scented oil, with which he anoints himself, and then receives the tooth, regarding it with deep and serious attention. Unbroken silence follows. The priest becomes absorbed in thought, and all eyes watch him with unblinking steadiness. In a few minutes he trembles; slight distortions are seen in his face, and twitching movements in his limbs. These increase to a violent muscular action, which spreads until the whole frame is strongly convulsed and the man shivers as with a strong ague fit. In some instances this is accompanied with murmurs and sobs, the veins are greatly enlarged, and the circulation of the blood quickened. The priest is now possessed by his god, and all his words and actions are considered as no longer his own, but those of the deity who has entered into him. Shrill cries of *"Koi au! Koi au!"* "It is I! It is I!" fill the air, and the god is supposed thus to notify his approach. While giving the answer, the priest's eyes stand out and roll as in a frenzy; his voice is unnatural, his face pale, his lips livid, his breathing depressed, and his entire appearance that of a furious madman. The sweat runs from every pore, and tears start from his strained eyes; after which the symptoms gradually disappear. The priest looks round with a vacant stare, and, as the god says, "I depart," announces his actual departure by violently flinging himself down on the mat, or by suddenly striking the ground with a club, when those at a distance are informed by blasts on the conch, or the firing of a musket, that the deity has returned into the world of spirits.

The Fijian gods are without number. Every island and village has its own divinities, and almost every individual has a private system of theology. The lonely dell, the gloomy cave, the desolate rock, and the deep forest, as well as the depths of the sea, are each peopled with invisible beings, many of them wicked and malicious. The trembling traveller is careful to cast a few leaves on the piles accumulated by the superstition of his predecessors, in the hope of inducing the deity to let them pass safely. The same motive of fear and desire to propitiate the gods actuates all their worship. The Fijian is not, strictly speaking, an idolater. The nearest approach he makes to idolatry is in reverencing certain consecrated stones and clubs, as well as some plants and animals,

Sacred Stones of Fiji.

Page 168.

supposed to contain deities. The distinction between the reverence thus paid, and worship, is perhaps a subtle one.

The Fijian gods are never represented by images; nor have they always shrines. The principal god is Ndengei. His origin is unknown, although his mother is said to lie at the bottom of a moat, in the shape of two great stones. The upper part of his body is said to be that of a serpent,—betokening his eternity; while the lower part is of stone, —emblematic of duration. His only sensation is hunger; his only movement, to turn over, which always produces an earthquake. Notwithstanding his supremacy over other gods, he exerts no influence over the affairs of men, and they pay him little homage. He has few temples on the islands, but at every feast his only attendant Uto is supposed to come for his master's share, which is usually a scanty one.

The other gods are numerous, and are described by Mr. Williams as "demonized heathen," every evil passion of the people being in them intensified.

Roko Mbati-Ndua, the "one-toothed lord," is in the shape of a man, with wings instead of arms, by means of which he flies through the air, emitting sparks of fire. His one tooth is fixed in his lower jaw; and on his wings are claws, which he uses to seize his victims.

The inferior gods are much alike in character, but each has some distinguishing peculiarities of person.

Kokola, for instance, has eight eyes; Matawalu, eight arms; Waluvakatini, eighty stomachs. Another has two bodies united, like the Siamese twins; and Thangawalu is a giant sixty feet high. These are but a few of an endless number.

The gods are divided into two classes, the highest immortal and divine, the lower composed of the spirits of chiefs and heroes, subject to many of the ills of life, and even to a second death. Admission into the latter order is easy. Said Tuikilakila to Mr. Hunt, "If you die first, I will make you my god."

The offerings made to the deities are almost all in supplication: sometimes, after a good season of turtle-fishing, or some remarkable escape from danger, they make the *madrali*, or *thank-offering;* but these instances are rare.

The offering is always in proportion to the importance of the boon desired. A *bure* is built only in cases of extraordinary consequence. Tuikilakila, the noted king of Somo-somo, earnestly desiring the assistance of the war-god, not only built him a large temple, but presented to him whales' teeth, sixty turtles, and a quantity of cooked food. Part of these gifts is set aside for the gods, in reality falling to the priests: the rest form a great feast, of which the whole tribe partake.

Cannibalism is part of the religious services of the Fijian. The gods—especially Ndengei—are supposed to be great cannibals; and the sacrifices to them are many. The inferior wives of chiefs used frequently to be offered for this purpose; but this practice is now checked.

The future state is believed by the Fijians to contain several divisions, adapted to the different merits of mortals.

Mburotu is the Elysium of the Fijian, where he expects to find all the delights to which he is most susceptible on earth. The inhabitants of that favored abode are believed to repose under the shade of sweet-scented groves, where the softest and most fragrant breezes fan them, where the skies are ever blue, and where no interruption to perfect peace and rest can come. One of their native songs shows their idea of simple rest in death, thus:—

> "Death is easy
> Of what use is life?
> To die is rest."

Mbulu is the general term for the world of departed spirits, to which a long and weary road is supposed to lead. In some parts of this abode the people are said to live much as they do on earth, but to be of much larger size than they were in this world.

The Fijians have no belief in future rewards or punishments, except that those who have displeased the gods will at some time surely feel their anger. Some offenders are supposed to be laid in rows and converted into taro-beds. Men who have not had their ears bored are condemned to carry the wooden log on which cloth is beaten, forever on their shoulders, scoffed at by all who see them. Women who have not slain an enemy in battle are sentenced to use the club neglected in life in beating a pile of filth, which is the most degrading punishment that can be inflicted upon a Fijian.

A spirit has many obstacles to encounter in an attempt to reach Mbulu. The cannibal gods watch eagerly for the souls of men, and each god has his own class of animate or inanimate objects appropriated to him. So numerous are the difficulties in the way that comparatively few are believed to have the happiness of entering Mbulu.

The journey a spirit has to take after death, before he can reach Mbulu, is long and dangerous. Mr. Williams gives in substance the following as the traditionary account of the path, modified in different localities:—
" The spirit first reaches a hill called Taki-veleyawa, which, however beautified with trees and flowers visible to spirits, to mortals

is dreary and desolate." Here he throws the whale's tooth, that was put in his hand after death, at the ghost of a pandanus-tree: if he succeeds in hitting this, he ascends the hill, and waits for his wife and other companions whom he expects to join him.

But if he should fail, he waits in vain for company, and pitifully laments, "How is this? For a long time I planted food for my wife, and it was also of great use to her friends: why, then, is she not allowed to follow me? Do my friends love me no better than this, after so many years of toil? Will no one, in love to me, strangle my wife?"

On the road to Mbulu is the town of Nambanggatai Samu, the killer of souls, and his brothers hide themselves in some spiritual mangrove bushes just beyond the town, and alongside of the path, in which they stick a reed as a prohibition to the spirit to pass that way. Should the comer be courageous, he raises his club in defiance of the *tabu* and those who placed it there; whereupon Samu appears to give him battle. Should the ghost conquer in the combat, he passes on to the judgment-seat; but, if wounded, he is doomed to wander among the mountains. If he be killed in the encounter, he is cooked and eaten by Samu and his brethren.

Those who escape the club of the soul-destroyer walk on to one of the highest peaks of the Kauvandra mountains. Here the path to Mbulu ends abruptly at the brink of a precipice, the base of which is said to be washed by a deep lake. Beyond this precipice projects a large oar, which tradition puts in the keeping of an old man and his son, who act under the direction of the god. These accost the coming spirit thus:—"Under what circumstances do you come to us? How did you conduct yourself in the other world?" If the ghost should be one of rank, he answers, "I am a great chief. I lived as a chief, and my conduct was that of a chief. I had great wealth, many wives, and ruled over a powerful people. I have destroyed many towns, and slain many in war." To this the reply is, "Good, good. Take a seat on the broad part of this oar, and refresh yourself in the cool breeze." No sooner is he seated, than they lift the handle of the oar, which lies inland, and he is thus thrown down headlong into the deep waters below, through which he passes to Murimuria. Such as have gained the special favor of Ndengei are warned not to go out on the oar, but to sit near those who hold it, and, after a short repose, are sent back to the place whence they came, to be deified.

The spirits of brutes, flowers, trees, and artificial objects, such as canoes, houses, &c., are believed by some to escape to the Mbulu paradise. On Vanua Levu it is believed that these fly by the same route taken by the spirits of men, but that they meet on the road a god who seizes them and appropriates them to his own use.

The Fijians believe that spirits return to earth and annoy mankind. Some speak of a man as having two spirits; his shadow, or "dark spirit," is the one that travels off to the world of shadows, while the other is his reflection in water or a looking-glass. The latter haunts the spot where he dies; and in rainy weather the people fancy they hear it moan as it sits with its head on its hands trying to relieve its misery.

So fearful are the natives of these ghosts that they often hide themselves after a death till they think the spirit is at rest. Thus are they made wretched by superstitions most puerile and senseless.

Witchcraft exercises over the Fijian people a more powerful influence than any other superstition. The modes of practising it are various, but the design is usually to destroy life. Men who laugh at the pretensions of the priest tremble at the power of the wizard; and those who become Christians lose this fear last of all the relics of their heathenism. The priests sometimes practise this art; but it is not confined to them. The natives purchase, at a high rate, the influence of the wizard, and they make offerings to the gods or the chiefs in order to avert the spell of witchcraft. So great is the dread of some of these charms, that persons have lain down and died from terror on learning that they were the objects of them.

One of the most fearful punishments that can be inflicted on a native is the *yalovaki*. When the evidence is strong against a person suspected of some offence, and yet he refuses to confess, the chief who is judge calls for a scarf, with which "to catch away the soul of the rogue." A threat of the rack could not be more effectual. The culprit generally confesses on the sight, and even the mention, of the light instrument: if not, it would be waved over his head until his soul was secured, and then carefully folded up and nailed to the small end of a chief's canoe; and, for want of his soul the suspected person would pine and die.

Those who have reason to suspect others of plotting against them avoid eating in their presence, or are careful to leave no fragment of food behind: they also dispose their garment so that no part can be removed. Most natives, on cutting their hair, hide what is cut off in the thatch of their own homes. Some build themselves a small house and surround it with a moat, believing that a little water will neutralize the charms which are directed against them.

There are various methods of divination used in Fiji. One is by a bunch of cocoa-nuts, pretty well dried. Having given the message of the god, the priest continues:—"I shall shake these nuts: if all fall off, the child will recover; but if any remain on, it will die." He then shakes and jerks the nuts, generally with all his might. Some pour a few drops of water on the front of the right arm, near the shoulder, and, the arm being gently inclined, the course of the water is watched; and if it find its way down to the wrist the answer is favorable, but otherwise if it run off and fall on the floor.

The seer also is known in Fiji. He sits listening to the applicant's wishes, and then, closing his eyes on earthly things, describes to the inquirer the scenes of the future which pass before his vision. These generally consist of burning houses, fleeing warriors, bloody plains, or death-stricken sick ones, as the case may require. A similar personage is the *taro,* "ask," who sits with his knee up and his foot resting on the heel, with a stick placed in a line with the middle of it. Without being told the object of the visit, he states whether his presentiment is good or evil, and then is informed of the matter inquired after, and proceeds to apply his impressions about it in detail. There is also the *dautadra,* or professional dreamer, who receives a present on communicating his revelations to the parties concerned, whether they tell of good or evil, and who seldom happens to dream about any one who cannot pay well. Some believe that a good present often averts the evil of a bad dream.

Their traditions are numerous and contradictory. One of these in regard to the origin of the races is similar to a tradition among the blacks of Africa. They say that the first person created was the Fijian; he was dark and badly behaved, so the gods punished him by giving him very little clothing; next they made the Tongan, who was lighter and better-behaved, so they gave him a better supply of apparel than the Fijian; the last one they formed was the white man, who was of such a fine color, and so good, that they rewarded him by giving him an ample suit.

Ndengei, according to one Fijian tradition, was the creator of man. He failed clumsily in several of his first attempts; and the first woman he made was met by the god Roko Matu, who was much displeased with her formation, and persuaded Ndengei to alter her to her present figure.

In the Fiji Islands we find the universal tradition of the flood. The natives have several different accounts of it, which agree in the main points. One of these tells us that Ndengei had two mischievous grandsons, who killed his favorite bird. Adding insolence and defiance to the outrage, they fortified the town in which they lived, and defied their grandfather to do his worst. He spent three months in gathering an army, but was not able to conquer the rebels. He then commanded the rain to fall, and the whole earth was flooded, houses and mountains were submerged; but the insurgents, from their rocky tower, looked defiantly down on the rising waters. But when they saw the waves reaching and invading their stronghold, they called in terror to a god, who directed them to build a boat, in which eight persons were saved.

When the waters subsided, they were left on Mbengga. From this circumstance the Mbenggans claim to be first in Fiji, their title signifying "subject only to heaven."

All of their histories of the flood agree with the biblical account in the number of persons saved, and in the belief that it was by supernatural interposition.

The highest point of the island of Koro is associated with the history of the flood. Its name is Ngginggi-tangithi-Koro, which conveys the idea of a little bird sitting there and lamenting the drowned island. In this bird the Christians recognize Noah's dove on its second flight from the ark. "I have heard a native," says Mr. Williams, "after listening to the incident as given by Moses, chant, '*Na qiqi sa tagici Koro ni yali:*'

'The Qiqi laments over Koro, because it is lost.'"

We find here also a trace of the tower of Babel:—"Near Na Savu, Vanua Levu, the natives point out the site where, in former ages, men built a vast tower, being eager for astronomic information, and especially anxious to decide the difficult question as to whether the moon was inhabited. To effect their purpose, they cast up a high mound, and erected thereon a great building of timber. The tower had already risen far skyward, and the ambitious hopes of its industrious builders seemed near fulfilment, when the lower fastenings suddenly broke asunder and scattered the workmen over every part of Fiji." These traditions are of much interest to the Christian world, however we may account for their striking similarity to Bible history and events. It cannot now be ascertained with certainty how these fragments of truth came to be interwoven with traditionary falsehoods; but the fact is a suggestive one.

An attempt has now been made to give an outline of the Fijian people, their habits of life and character, their religious belief, and the main influences that operate to make them what the missionaries find them on reaching their shores.

It will be interesting to turn from this picture, and see what success those missionaries have had, by the blessing of God, in changing their habits, substituting the glorious light of the gospel for the gross darkness of heathenism, and raising them from moral degradation to virtue and decency. We may thus be led to wonder and adore, in view of the power of the Christian religion to enter the darkest soul and transform it into a soul washed white in the blood of the Lamb.

The Cannibal Islands.

PART II.

FIJI RECEIVING THE GOSPEL.

"Hear the word of the Lord, O ye nations, and declare it in the isles afar off."

PART SECOND.

CHAPTER I.

THE MISSION ESTABLISHED.

The mission to the Fiji Islands has been as remarkable for its success as any ever undertaken by the Christian world. The account which has been given of the people exhibits faintly the difficulties that the gospel had to meet and conquer in order to make progress in its work. The darkest qualities of the Fijian nature—those which oppose the greatest barrier to the influence of Christianity—have been least noticed in that account. These facts should be considered in judging of the missionaries' labor.

Missionaries were sent to the Friendly Islands, another group in the Pacific, as early as 1796; but for nearly twenty years they wearily labored, cheered by no success. Still they toiled, and waited for the blessing, in the confidence that these islands were to be eventually converted to God. Nor did they wait in vain. A history of this successful mission has been published, showing what was wrought by God among these savage islanders.

The influence of the missionaries extended gradually to the Fiji Islands, in consequence of the frequent visits made by Tongans to them. These visits were sometimes involuntary, owing to the drifting of their canoes in that direction, and sometimes made to obtain timber or to trade in various articles. The Fijian timber was especially desired; and a number of those visiting the islands for this or other purposes finally obtained a footing there and made permanent settlements. Some few of these Tongan sailors had been converted to Christ in their own islands; and when they found themselves among those yet ignorant of the Saviour, they sought to shed the light given to them upon the darkness around; and thus was Christianity first brought to Fiji.

THE MISSION ESTABLISHED.

But in 1834, when the Tongan Church was visited with a remarkable blessing from God, the first-fruits of the new life begun in them were manifested in an earnest desire to attempt in a more direct manner the spreading of the "tidings of great joy" in the Fijian Islands. Small as the number of missionaries was in the Friendly Islands, they determined, after earnest, prayerful consultation together, to send two of the little band to Fiji.

The Rev. William Cross and Rev. David Cargill were appointed to undertake this mission. It was not a small sacrifice which these men made in leaving the scene of their past labors for a new and perilous field. Mr. Cross had been eight years, and Mr. Cargill two, in the Friendly Islands, and they had established homes, had become attached to the people, and began to see the fruit of all their toil and suffering. But immortal souls cried out to them from the neighboring darkness and wretchedness of savage heathenism, asking for the light of life; and the call could not be unheeded.

The two missionaries, with their families, sailed October 8, 1835, and reached Lakemba October 12, having before their departure begun to study the language, constructed an alphabet, and printed in Fijian a little "First book" and a catechism.

The Christian king George of Tonga sent to accompany them an influential person, with a present to the King of Lakemba, and a message stating the benefits conferred by the missionaries on himself and his people and urging their kind treatment of them.

Lakemba is one of the largest islands in the eastern part of the group. It is thirty miles in circumference, and has twelve towns upon it, containing in all about four thousand inhabitants.

Early in the morning, the two missionaries went ashore in a boat, the schooner in the mean time lying off without coming to anchor. Deafening shouts along the shore announced the approach of the vessel, and drew together a great crowd of wild-looking Tongans and Fijians, armed and blackened, according to their custom, to receive the strangers.

At the very outset, the missionaries had a great advantage in being able at once to converse with the people without an interpreter; for many of the Fijians at Lakemba, through very long intercourse with the Tongans, could speak their language. Thus the visitors passed through crowds of Tongans, hailing them with the friendly greetings of their own land; and leaving behind them the Tongan houses, stretching for nearly half a mile among the cocoanut-trees on the shore, they came at once to the king's town, which lies about four hundred yards inland. In one of his large houses, they were introduced to the king and some of his chiefs. Tui Nayau readily promised them land for the mission premises, and desired that their families and goods should be landed forthwith, promising that temporary houses should be erected as soon as possible. In the mean time, one of his own large houses was offered to the strangers, who, however, feared to reside within the town, considering it unhealthy from its crowded state and the embankment and moat by which it is surrounded.

The interview was very favorable, and, a suitable place having been chosen for the new dwellings, between the town and the Tongan settlement, the missionaries returned to the schooner to give in their report to their wives and the captain. The "Blackbird" then cast anchor, and the families, who had suffered very severely from sea-sickness, were only too eager to get ashore. A large canoe-house on the beach, open at the sides and end, was given them as their dwelling until proper houses could be built. Under this great shed the two families passed the night, but not in sleep. The curtains had been left on board with their other goods; and they speak of the mosquitos that night as being "innumerable and unusually large." Numbers of pigs, too, seemed greatly disquieted, and kept up a loud grunting all round until morning. Here, then, beneath a canoe-shed, the missionary band spent their first night in Fiji, the wives and children

THE MISSION ESTABLISHED. 193

worn out with their voyage, stung by numberless mosquitos, and the crying of the little ones answered by the grunts of pigs running about in all directions. Glad enough were they, the next morning, to accept the captain's invitation and go back to the vessel until their houses were ready.

House-building is sharp work in Fiji. The missionaries arrived at Lakemba on the 12th, the houses were commenced on the 14th, and on the 17th the two families took possession of them. They were told by the king that these houses were only temporary houses, till he could erect substantial buildings for their use.

The next day was the Sabbath, and the missionaries preached twice out-of-doors in the Tongan language to about one hundred and fifty Tongans and Fijians. In the morning King Tui Nayau attended, and listened very attentively. The missionaries soon found abundant occupation for hands, head, and heart. Hands must be busy in completing the houses and putting up doors and windows; the language must be studied, the Scriptures translated, and a grammar and dictionary commenced.

Their numerous occupations were constantly interrupted by the visits of the natives, who came to trade with or to stare at the strangers, and usually to secrete and carry away any small articles they could find. This influx of visitors was annoying to the missionaries; but, as it brought them into familiar contact with the natives, it could not be altogether discouraged.

It was frequently the case that large parties visiting Lakemba from distant islands would ask permission to inspect the premises, which was generally granted. These visitors, having nothing to do, were generally disposed to stay longer than was necessary for any good purpose, and would prowl about, picking up any knife or other small article that they could lay hands on, and secreting it, with marvellous cleverness, in their scanty clothing. Increased watchfulness was the result; and such parties, after having spent time enough in examining the place, and having listened with attention to a state-

THE MISSION ESTABLISHED. 195

ment of the objects of the mission, were informed that the missionary or his wife had other business, and were kindly reminded of the expediency of their attending to their own affairs elsewhere.

Considerable losses and much annoyance, but great good also, came of all this. The natives took notice of every thing, and could not help admiring the domestic comforts, regularity of meals, subjection of children, love of husband and wife, and general social enjoyment, which could only be taught by a practical exhibition of them in every day-life.

The only way in which the missionaries could obtain necessary food or services, such as gardening, fencing, &c., was by exchanging for them knives, axes, calicoes, and other articles desired by the natives. Whatever the mission families needed was bargained for in the same manner, thus stimulating the industry of the people and introducing civilized comforts among them.

The king's promise to build for the mission more substantial dwellings was still unfulfilled, when one day a hurricane blew the two houses down, and Tui Nayau could delay no longer the erection of new buildings for the *Papalangis*. In addition he built them a chapel, using the posts and timber of the ruined houses for the purpose. While the comfort of the mission families was thus more permanently secured, much additional labor was brought upon them for a time in arranging and furnishing their dwellings and chapel.

When the new year came in, they had in their chapel a regular congregation of about two hundred persons. In the spring thirty-one adults and twenty-three children were baptized, classes for church-members formed, and a school for all ages organized. Of the thirty-one adults just mentioned, the majority were Tongans. These people, who had been notoriously wicked even in Fiji, were some of them so manifestly changed from savage heathen into gentle, self-denying Christians as to render invaluable service to the mission work among the Fijians. Their independent position among

THE MISSION ESTABLISHED. 197

the Fijians made their profession a bold one; and they afterwards spread the knowledge of the gospel to other islands with earnestness and zeal. The Fijians around them did not fail to see the change wrought in them and to be in time influenced by it in their own lives.

Gradually the number of visitors to the mission premises increased and attracted the attention of the authorities by their discontent with their own gods and priests and their refusal to comply with their demands. Those in favor of the new religion were for a time protected from violence by the fact that a Tongan chief whose party were powerful for the defence of Lakemba was a convert to Christianity. But the king's god, and the priests in the name of the gods, were loud in their denunciations of the missionaries, their doctrines, and their converts; and an attack was finally made upon the houses of the Christians and their possessions. As is always the case, however, the true religion gained instead of losing ground by these measures. The calm and steadfast endurance by the Christians of persecution, and their willingness to shed their blood in defence of their new faith, at the same time that they manifested kindness and good will towards the king, impressed their enemies most forcibly and favorably. Attention was more drawn to the missionaries and their teachings, and the claims of the native priests were more closely examined, resulting in the discovery of many failures on their part to prophesy truly and to fulfil their promises of aid.

While the priests were thus losing the confidence of the people, the missionaries were daily acquiring more influence over them, by their ability to supply them with desired articles and to give them help in many ways. At the end of a year there was a church of two hundred and eighty persons; there was regular preaching in four towns, and day-schools, Scripture readers, and written, as well as a few printed, books.

The domestic affairs of the missionary families were at this time painfully embarrassed. Their articles for barter were all gone, and these were their only means of obtaining fresh food. They were obliged, therefore, for several months to use musty flour; and when that too was gone, their subsistence was on yams and salt, and cakes made of arrow-root and yams. The health of some of them suffered from their privations. Calicoes, sorely wanted for family use, were parted with to obtain food. Trunks, wearing-apparel, and every thing else available, were thus disposed of. Mere conveniences, such as cooking-utensils or crockery-ware, had disappeared: so that Mr. Cargill had only one teacup left, and that had lost its handle. This state of things lasted until the end of the year, when an opportunity at last came of sending help from Tonga.

During this year of domestic trial, letters and a vessel of supplies arrived, and gave much joy and relief. As the sloop was leaving Lakemba, it was wrecked; but the crew were saved, and in a few days returned to Lakemba. Before Christianity was known in Fiji, shipwrecked men were killed and eaten; but its humanizing influence now caused them to be unmolested.

The captain, mate, and supercargo were received by the missionaries, and, in return for the kindness shown by their entertainers, the sailors made stools, bedsteads, and other useful articles of furniture, from wreckage picked up by the natives. Mr. Cargill at last reached such a degree of luxury as to have part of the floor of his bedroom boarded, whereby much more comfort was secured than by mats.

From time to time supplies of clothing and stores reached the mission families; but they labored with prostrating sickness often among them, and amidst difficulties and trials of which Christians at home know little. The news of results reached England; but little could be said, and nothing realized, of the weariness, the disappointment, the sufferings and tears, which these men, accustomed to comfort, had undergone for themselves and their families before such news could be told.

At the close of 1837 the missionaries decided to carry the gospel to another part of the Fijian group, and Mr. Cross, with his family, removed to Mbau. Here, in a small damp house, containing but one room, the missionary was taken ill, and for many weeks was apparently on the verge of the grave. He recovered with shattered health, and began his labors with a good prospect of success. Persecution came, and, as at Lakemba, first checked, then fostered, the growth of the new religion.

At both the Fijian mission stations help was now needed most sorely by the two solitary laborers; and this need was realized in the Friendly Islands. An earnest appeal was successfully addressed to Christians in England in behalf of Fiji, and three missionaries were at once sent from that country, to be joined by two more from the Friendly Islands. The Rev. John Hunt, T. J. Jagger, and James Calvert sailed from England in April, 1838, and Mr. Lyth and Mr. Spinney afterwards joined them at Fiji. Mr. Hunt went immediately to Rewa, for the purpose of relieving Mr. Cross from part of his labors; and, as he carried with him good stores for barter, his arrival added much to the comfort of the mission. There was enough to encourage the missionaries in what they saw around them as the results of their labors. The attention of the people was awakened, many forsook their priests and temples for the mission church, and some gave evidence of being truly renewed in heart and life. Cannibalism and other savage horrors were still practised, almost within sight of the missionaries; but they knew that the true religion had taken deep root, and that it would grow and spread until its blessed influence should cover the land and transform its moral barrenness into spiritual life and beauty.

A great event had in the mean time taken place in Lakemba. The expected printing-press had arrived in good order, had been set up, and the Gospel of St. Mark and the catechism had been printed in Fijian. Three years before, no written language existed on the islands, and the degraded inhabitants knew not the darkness in which they lived. Now the instrument of enlightenment, of civilization, and of power was at work among them, and their condition could never be quite so low as it had been. The missionaries now felt that they had a sufficiently effective force to extend their labors to other islands in the group. They resolved to remove the printing-press to Rewa, as being the best fitted for a central station, and to establish two new stations. Soon afterwards Mr. Spinney arrived from the Friendly Islands; but it was only to leave Fiji again immediately for Sydney, to check, if possible, the progress of far-advanced disease. He died in the February following; and his loss was deeply felt by the little band of laborers for the Lord in Fiji.

CHAPTER II.

ONO.

THE island of Ono is the chief of a small group in the south of Fiji. It is tributary to Lakemba, and is about one hundred and fifty miles distant from it. There is considerable traffic, and a friendly state of feeling, between the two places.

During the year 1835—the same year that Mr. Cross and Mr. Cargill came to Fiji, but previous to their arrival—Wai, a chief from Ono, visited Lakemba to bring the annual tribute. His people had been recently suffering from destructive wars and a raging epidemic, which had caused great and widespread alarm. They redoubled their zeal in worshipping and offering sacrifices to their gods, but no help or relief came. In this distress Wai left them to go to Lakemba. There he met Takai, a chief who had visited the Friendly Islands and Tahiti and become a Christian. This man told Wai all he knew of the true God, which was that there was but one God, and Jehovah was his name, and that it was wrong to worship any other. Carrying this precious gleam of gospel light with him, Wai returned to his dark and sorrowing land. He and the companions of his journey had now lost all faith in the native gods; and they determined to forsake them and pray to Jehovah for help in their distress. Resolving to conduct every thing as nearly as possible after the manner of the Christians, they set aside the seventh day for the worship of God. Their food was prepared on the previous day, they dressed with extraordinary care, anointed their bodies profusely, and met to join in Christian worship. But when they were assembled, a difficulty presented itself. They knew they should pray to Jehovah; but no one of them had ever tried to pray: the priests had always done that for them. In their perplexity they now appealed to one of their heathen priests for assistance.

The priest consented—from fear or kindness—to officiate for them; and this group of heathens *felt after* " the Lord, if haply they might find him," in these words uttered by the priest:—" Lord Jehovah! here are thy people: they worship thee. I turn my back on thee for the present, and am on another tack, worshipping another god. But do thou bless these thy people: keep them from harm, and do them good."

After this brief service the people returned

to their usual occupations, and on every seventh day they met to worship Jehovah, with the priest for their minister.

Nor was the merciful God unmindful of their prayer; for in their hearts he strengthened the desire to know more of him, and opened the way for its fulfilment.

The people, as they looked eagerly for an opportunity to obtain the knowledge for which they thirsted, hailed with unusual delight the arrival of a whaler which stopped at Ono for provision on its way to the Friendly Islands. This vessel agreed to take two messengers to Tonga, where the people knew that missionaries were stationed, to beg for a teacher.

The Lord did not suffer these earnest, simple-hearted inquirers after truth to wait the long time necessary for a voyage to Tonga and back.

That spring a company of Christian Tongans set sail from Lakemba for Tonga. The winds were contrary, the canoe became unmanageable, and they drifted off to Vatoa, or Turtle Island, about fifty miles from Ono.

Here they found that the new religion at Ono was the universal topic of conversation; and this subject was one of deep interest to the shipwrecked Christians. One of them—a young man, Josiah by name—hastened to go to Ono and tell them all he could of the God they were so earnestly seeking.

In the mean time the two messengers arrived at Tonga, where they were told that there were now two missionaries in Fiji, at Lakemba, and that they must apply to them. They went directly home with this intelligence; but their astonishment was great when they saw the changes that had taken place during their absence. Instead of the heathen priest who had prayed to Jehovah, "worshipping another god," was the Christian Josiah conducting public services and teaching all who came to him. Some of the people were praying for themselves; the whole of the Sabbath was kept holy; a chapel was built, and the number of worshippers had increased to forty. The news their messengers brought of missionaries being so near them aroused an ardent desire in the minds of the people to have a teacher fully qualified to administer all the rites of the Christian religion; but they knew that the voyage to Lakemba was long and perilous, and the teachers were few. Yet the Lord they sought was again watching over and providing for them in a way they knew not. A young man of Ono, wild and reckless, who had gone to Tonga some years before, had there become a Christian, and joined the missionaries at Lakemba, where he labored with energy in order to qualify himself to teach among his own people. The missionaries instructed and assisted him until he was fitted to be a preacher, when they sent him to Ono. He took the name of Isaac Ravuata. His arrival at Ono was in the beginning of 1838; and he found that already one hundred and twenty adults had forsaken idolatry for the worship of the true God, and that they were living quiet, well-ordered lives. They received him most joyfully, supplied him with every thing for his comfort, and eagerly opened their hearts to his teaching of gospel truth.

Isaac soon found that he needed books, and sent word by the returning canoe to tell the missionaries of this want. When the message reached them, Mr. Cargill's time was fully occupied with preaching four times on Sunday and several times through the week, translating the Scriptures, visiting the towns, and constantly interrupted by visitors: yet, with the assistance of his wife, he prepared a number of elementary books and sent them to Ono.

From Ono the missionaries still received good tidings. In 1839 they sent thither three more teachers; and the sailors who took them brought back an entreaty for a missionary, and also the intelligence that the number of converts had increased to three hundred and twenty-eight. They had built three chapels, all of which were well filled; and the people were so anxious to be taught that they would scarcely allow the teachers time to take the needful rest from their labors. The same canoe returning to Lakemba brought news that the little island of Vatoa—Turtle Island—had also received the glad tidings of the gospel. A Vatoan had been converted at Lakemba, and on his return home persuaded his people to forsake their gods: so that when the Lakemba Christians left Vatoa the whole number of inhabitants—sixty-six—professed Christianity and urgently requested a teacher.

CHAPTER III.

REWA.

WHILE the people in Lakemba were yielding to the influence of the new religion, the king Tui Nayau was becoming more open in his expressions of hostility to the converts. He still, however, avowed his belief in Christianity and his intention of embracing it, saying that he was only hindered from taking that step by his fear of more powerful chiefs. He desired the missionaries to go to some more powerful chief and persuade him to take the lead.

The missionaries, anxious to extend their efforts, determined to follow the king's advice, insincere as it was. Their stock for barter was so reduced that they scarcely knew how they could build houses and procure food in a new place; but Mr. Cross, notwithstanding these difficulties and his ill health, resolved to go to Mbau.

This island was fast becoming the centre of political power,—which important position it has since occupied. "A seven-years civil war had just passed its crisis," and Tanoa, the old Fijian king, had been driven out of his kingdom. His young son Seru was permitted to remain.

The character of the young prince was not at all comprehended by the people; but there was one old chief of Viwa who said that he would prove dangerous, and advised that he should be put to death. At this counsel the others merely laughed, saying they could not imagine what evil a mere boy like Seru could do.

Seru was in secret correspondence with his father, who supplied him with property that he distributed among the people. He succeeded in winning over many, among whom was his most intimate friend Verani, the nephew of the shrewd Viwa chief.

They laid their plans so well that the rebels were conquered. Tanoa returned; and a grand cannibal feast in honor of the victory was in full operation when Mr. Cross and his family arrived.

Seru, or Shakombau (Evil to Mbau), as he was now called, met them, and told them it would be much better for them to go to Rewa for the present: Mbau was still in a state of intense excitement: the king of Rewa would protect them and give them land, and was willing to allow his people to *lotu,* or, embrace Christianity.

This advice was so good that Mr. Cross took it.

Rewa is next in importance to Mbau, and only twelve miles distant. Here Mr. and Mrs. Cross landed on the 8th of January, 1838. They were kindly received, a small house was given them, and they were now fairly alone among the cannibals.

They had been here but a short time when Mr. Cross was taken sick, first with intermittent fever, then followed by cholera; and finally the typhus fever attacked him, and he seemed to be dying. His wife and little children could help him but little. David Whippy, an American settled at Ovalau, heard of their deplorable condition, and went to their aid. Mr. Cross gradually recovered: the king built him a larger and more comfortable house, and all began to look brighter.

A chief and his wife now became Christians, and opened their house for worship, which before had been held out-of-doors,— making an agreeable change. A school was next established. The king was their zealous protector; but, in spite of his care, many attempts were made on Mr. Cross's life: stones were thrown in at him during church-hours, and once they endeavored to burn down the house.

If the king could not protect Mr. Cross, his Master could; and he was preserved from all their malicious designs.

Na-mosi-malua, chief of Viwa, and the same who advised Seru's death, was now at peace with Mbau, and was very desirous of having a teacher.

Mr. Cross did not know what to do about it. From the chief's character, and from his having recently been severely punished, having his town burned down and his crops spoiled by the French for having captured a French brig and murdered the captain and most of the crew, Mr. Cross feared that it was but a scheme of Na-mosi-malua's to revenge himself on the whites.

But Tanoa strongly advised it: the Viwa chief had told him he was going to *lotu*, for he was afraid of the Papalangis. So Mr. Cross sent a native teacher, and Na-mosi-malua built a large chapel, where he and many of his people worshipped. Thus Christianity stepped from island to island, extending its influence in this savage group.

CHAPTER IV.

SOMO-SOMO.

Somo-somo was one of the new stations established in 1839. It is a town of great importance, and its king, with two sons and a number of his people, had visited Lakemba soon after the missionaries went there, and urged very strongly their claim for a mission station. The useful articles obtained by the Lakembans from the mission house gave these people an undue advantage, it was declared, over their more powerful neighbors; and the king promised welcome and attention to their teaching if the missionaries only would come to them. The extensive influence of this king and his sons, and the fear in which they were held, induced the missionaries to promise to send some one to them; and in fulfilment of that agreement Mr. Hunt and Mr. Lyth went to Somo-somo in July, 1839.

They soon found they were to become conversant with the most horrible customs of Fiji. Somo-somo was noted for its atrocities, and particularly for its cannibalism; and the missionaries found this reputation a deserved one. Although the people had been so anxious to have them come, they paid them no attention after their arrival, and seemed perfectly indifferent to their teaching. The king's great house was given them as a residence, and the people were very willing to bring fruits and vegetables for them to buy; but further than this little heed was given to them. Greater troubles soon came upon them.

When they arrived, they found the people expecting the return of Ra Mbithi, the king's youngest son, who had gone with a fleet of canoes to the windward islands. After the missionaries had got all their goods landed, and before the vessel in which they came had left, tidings reached Somo-somo that Ra Mbithi had been lost at sea. The ill news caused terrible excitement in the town, and, according to custom, several women were at once set apart to be strangled. The missionaries began their work by pleading for the lives of these wretched victims. The utmost they could effect was to get the execution delayed until the schooner should have gone to search for the young chief and bring back further information. The vessel returned, but not with any more favorable news. Now a greater number of women were condemned; and again the missionaries pleaded hard that they might be spared. The old king was angry with the strangers for presuming to interfere with the affairs of his people, and indignant at the thought of his favorite son dying without the customary honors. Once more, however, the strangling was put off. Canoes which had been sent out to search at last returned, bringing the intelligence that all was true. It was generally known, though not talked about, that Ra Mbithi had drifted on his wrecked canoe to the island of Ngau, where he had been captured and eaten by the natives. Remonstrance and entreaty were now in vain. Sixteen women were forthwith strangled in honor of the young chief and his companions, and the bodies of the principal women were buried within a few yards of the missionaries' door.

Such were the scenes which met the missionaries on the threshold of their work at Somo-somo. Tuithakau, the old king, was a horrible cannibal, but disposed to be friendly to the missionaries. Tuikilakila, his son, was, on the contrary, an open enemy to them. This man was tall, broad, and perfectly black,—a true specimen of the untamed savage. He was in the habit of strolling through the mission premises as he pleased; and the two ladies, to their intense annoyance, often found him in their rooms arranging his toilet.

The servants of the missionaries one day brought them the news that two dead men were being brought from Lauthala. They hardly knew how to understand this; for they had been too short a time in Fiji to become familiar with cannibalism. But very soon *eleven* bodies, instead of two, were brought and laid close by the mission house as materials for a feast.

The windows and doors were tight.y closed, to exclude the disgusting sight and smell; but Mr. Hunt, standing in his yard, witnessed the horrible ceremonies.

After the feast was over, Tuikilakila came and knocked at the door, and demanded of Mr. Hunt, who opened it, why the windows were closed.

"Because," answered Mr. Hunt, "we wish to shut out your horrible wickedness."

"If you do so again," replied the ferocious cannibal, unmindful of the presence of Mrs. Hunt and Mrs. Lyth, "I'll knock you in the head and then eat you!"

From threats the natives proceeded to attempt actual violence. Tuikilakila came one day, club in hand, to kill Mr. Lyth, who had refused to purchase part of a melon from the king's favorite wife. Mr. Lyth fled to his bedroom, while Mr. Hunt talked to the enraged chief till his anger cooled down.

At last it became evident that the people were preparing to put into execution their many threats; and one night the end seemed at hand. The missionaries had reason to believe that the people had gathered to murder them and their helpless families. In the great gloomy house where the missionaries lived, with thick mosquito-nets hung up to prevent the natives from peeping in through the reed walls, this little band betook themselves to prayer. They looked at the death before them. They saw beyond it, laid up for them in heaven, crowns of gold, purchased by the Saviour's blood. To die to them was gain, and they were content with a martyr's death. Although husbands and wives looked at each other and at their little ones and realized the horrors of their situation, yet in this hour of danger they were ready on their knees in prayer to complete in death the sacrifice they had begun by leaving homes and country.

At midnight, while they were praying, a wild shout rang through the air, and each head bent lower in anticipation of their enemies' instant approach. But it proved to be the cry of their deliverance. The people had changed their purpose; and the cry they heard was a call to the women to come to a dance.

Their lives were now comparatively safe; but the daily trials they endured, and the violent opposition they encountered, were undiminished.

In 1840, Captain—now Admiral—Wilkes, of the United States Navy, stopped at Somo-somo. He expressed great sympathy for the missionaries, and offered to take them to any part of Fiji whither they might desire to remove; but they were unwilling as yet to leave the work which they had begun in Somo-somo. His admiration and respect were greatly excited by the devotion and faith of these Christians; but he doubted their success being at all "adequate to their exertions." The report of the missionaries at this time alludes, in passing, to the trials incident to their situation here; it tells of the many strangers who while visiting Somo-somo had heard the gospel, and states that Tuikilakila had permitted the preaching, but prevented any open result from it by threatening to kill the first one who should profess the new religion. But the first one was his uncle, a chief of great influence; and he dared not kill him. The chief's motive was that he might be cured from a dangerous sickness. The medical skill of the missionaries gained great credit to their religion; for the people thought there must be something in the religion itself to cure disease.

Although their congregations were small and their converts few, the two missionaries were not without encouragement to believe that they accomplished some good. At one time Tuikilakila was very sick, and all the native remedies, the doctors, and the gods, failed to do him any good. Mr. Lyth, who had been educated as a physician, offered to attend him, and did so successfully. Tuikilakila was won by the kindness of Mr. Lyth, and never forgot his obligations to him.

The old king, too, took a great fancy to him, and would often send food to the mission-house,—expecting, however, occasional

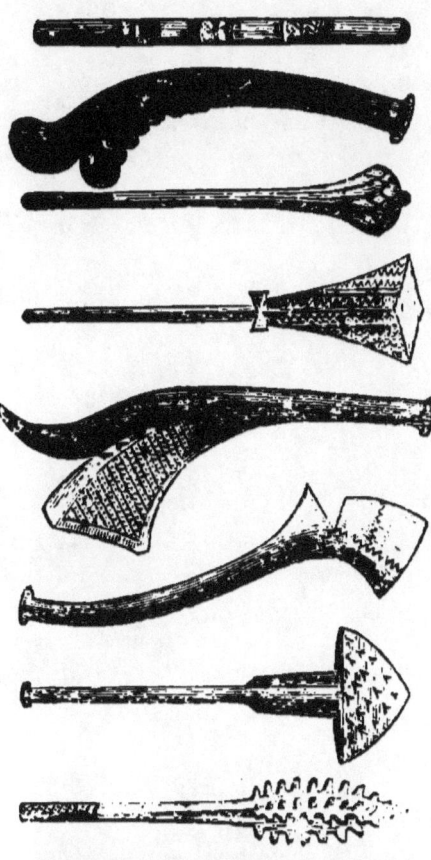

Fijian Clubs.

gifts of knives, iron pots, &c. Once, when the old man was ill, Mr. Lyth, in anxious concern about his salvation, spoke more pointedly than before, declaring that the gods of Somo-somo were no gods, and could do him no good. On being urged to turn to the true God, the mildness and friendship of this "virtuous heathen" forthwith vanished, and, seizing the missionary's coat, he called loudly for a club to kill him. The old chief was ill, but his rage made him dangerous, and he clung hard; but luckily the garment was of light material, and Mr. Lyth, making a spring, left his coat-tail in the hand of Tuithakau, and, without taking his hat, set off home, where he quietly waited until his patient's anger had cooled down. And here for the present we leave Mr. Hunt and Mr. Lyth, patiently working on amidst discouragement and trial, yet seeing some fruit of their labors in the changed lives of a few of those around them.

go to Viwa. Mr. Cross found that Na-mosi-malua had made every preparation possible to give him a comfortable home in Viwa, and was, moreover, ready to give him every assistance in his missionary work. Thakombau, with angry jealousy, kept a strict watch on all these things. He hated the chief and the Christian religion, and it did not please him to see the latter establishing itself upon an island so near and so powerful.

Viwa and the neighboring islands were visited by an epidemic a few weeks after Mr. Cross's arrival. Thakombau sent a messenger to the chief of Viwa to say that "the gods have sent this sickness on you and your people because you were unfaithful to them. Throw away the *lotu*, and I will come and help you rebuild the great *bure* for the Viwa god." But Na-mosi-malua answered, "Tell Thakombau that Jehovah alone is God; and Him alone I will continue to worship."

Thakombau had a faithful and powerful friend in Viwa, Verani, the nephew of Na-mosi-malua, and this man was united with him in opposition to Christianity. But now Verani, seeing it firmly established in his own island, began to consider this new religion more carefully; he conversed often with Mr. Cross on the subject, and excited hope in the minds of the converts that he would himself embrace their faith.

Thakombau entreated Verani to be firm in his enmity to Christianity, and promised him his aid if he would rebuild the temples. Verani was persuaded to remain a heathen, and he rebuilt the principal *bure*. But, although he was outwardly unconverted, his heart was not satisfied with heathenism.

Mr. Cross was now living quite comfortably. Tanoa, the Mbau king, was still friendly, and begged him to let him know whenever he wanted food, that he might send him some from Mbau. Among the many visitors to the mission-house, Thakombau soon made his appearance, and at his first visit stayed four hours, disputing with Mr. Cross about religious truth. As he left, he declared that he would never *lotu*,—

that is, embrace Christianity. "If you do not, your children will," said Mr. Cross. "Nay," replied the other: "though other places may, I will not; and when I am about to die I will tell my children not to *lotu*."

About this time Mbau engaged in war, and Na-mosi-malua was asked to help, but refused. Verani, with quite a large number of his people, joined heartily in it. The missionary work was now carried on amidst the tumult and noise of war. Schools were by this time established, many of the converts had learned to read, and the visitors constantly coming spread the knowledge of the true religion far and near. Constant applications were made for teachers, who were sent to as many places as possible. The chief wife of Verani was among the converts, and her husband gave her permission to *lotu*; but she refused to make any profession until he did.

During this year a small party of Viwan Christians were sailing close to the shore of the large island of Viti Levu, when the outrigger of their canoe broke. The people on shore, as soon as they saw the accident, ran eagerly to seize on the canoe and cargo, and to secure the crew for a cannibal feast, according to their custom. When they were near enough to see that the canoe was from Viwa, revenge increased their eagerness; for only a short time previous several of their friends had been murdered by Viwans. Hundreds of armed men assembled on the reef near the canoe, which lay tossed about in danger of being capsized at any moment, while the people on board worked hard to keep her right, and prayed earnestly to the Almighty to save them from the hands of their enemies, who, with brandished weapons, cried out,—

"You are in our power! Now we will kill you in return for the murder of our friends!"

A young man of the company cried to them, "Kill us if you wish; but know that we did not kill your friends. Before they were killed, we were Christians; and since that we have left off doing such evil deeds. It will be better for you not to kill us, but come and help us bale the water out of our canoe." This answer restrained the anger of the heathen, and some of them even went out to the canoe, helped them to bale it out and lash the outrigger, so that the canoe could safely sail away! Heathens who heard of it said, "It is Jehovah! for nothing like this was ever known in Fiji before."

Na-mosi-malua was certainly much changed in his outward life by his new religion. He was now a remarkably kind and peaceful man,—though his former excessive craftiness caused his motives still to be somewhat doubted. He had not been admitted into the church; for he yet had several wives, and it was a rule, strictly enforced, that a man professing Christianity should have but one wife, and be married to her by a religious service.

Thakombau at last persuaded Na-mosi-malua to assist him in a war with the town of Mathuata, which had neglected to pay the customary tribute to Mbau. During this war Na-mosi-malua manifested the merciful principles of Christianity in such a striking manner as to excite the astonishment of the heathen, and the displeasure of Thakombau, who exclaimed,—

"Christianity is powerful. Because of it we cannot get any men to eat!"

And it was remarkable that for several months not a single man had been eaten at Mbau.

Verani had promised that when he returned home from this expedition he and his wife would *lotu*. Thakombau's influence over him was so great, however, that he could not resolve to take the step. When he was reminded of his promise, and of the dangers through which he had passed, he said,—

"Yes; a ball went through my dress, and several came very near me. I prayed to the true God in my heart, and kept the Sabbath day when I was engaged in war.".

Mr. Cross was carefully watching for an opportunity to obtain a footing in Mbau, either for himself or for a teacher; but Thakombau's vigilance prevented. At last an opening seemed to be made. Viekoso, a brother of King Tanoa, had become a Christian at Viwa, where he had long resided; and, as he was now about to return to Mbau, a teacher was sent with him to conduct worship in his family and try to benefit the people. Thakombau saw danger in this, and, being in reality the king, he ordered his uncle to renounce his religion, and sent the teacher from the island.

CHAPTER VI.

LAKEMBA.

After the arrival of Mr. Hunt and his companions, and the subsequent distribution of the mission forces, Mr. Calvert was left alone at Lakemba. At this station they now had two hundred and thirty-eight members of the church, with many more on trial and in the schools. They had a chapel, which was capable of holding five hundred persons. The circuit of Lakemba consisted of thirteen towns on Lakemba, and twenty-four surrounding islands, at distances varying from eighteen to a hundred and forty miles.

Mr. Calvert had been in Fiji only six months, and was not acquainted with the people or the language; so that no ordinary amount of energy and zeal was needed for him to carry on the mission work alone. The thieving propensities of the natives made it difficult to keep clothing, household utensils, or articles of barter. Finally, one night they cut a hole through the reed wall of the house and stole fifty articles of wearing-apparel. They fortunately disturbed none of the sleeping inmates; for had any of them been awakened they would have been silenced by stones from a pile of stones the burglars had been accumulating for use.

Mr. Cargill determined to show the natives his love for them, by caring for their bodies as well as their souls; and for this end he visited them frequently at their houses, and mingled much with them. This course of conduct soon brought about beneficial results at Lakemba, as it afterwards did everywhere through the islands, so that soon Mr. Cargill reported,—

"We are now free from robberies and insult, and live in great peace: your missionaries and cause are respected by the chief and natives: so that the mission appears to have obtained a firm and permanent establishment here."

Tui Nayau was, in the mean time, secretly opposing Christianity, while Toki, his brother, was doing the same openly. Mr. Calvert suspected the state of affairs, and went one day to the king, telling him that he wished to have an understanding with him on the subject of the *lotu;* that two persons at the town of Nasangkalu had renounced heathenism, and others desired to do the same; and he begged permission for any so disposed to be allowed to become Christians without molestation. He assured the king that, so far from the Christians failing in due respect, tribute, or labor, they would be taught that it was their duty to obey the laws in these matters.

Both of the chiefs said that Christianity was "a very good thing," and promised that the people should be free to worship God if they pleased. Mr. Calvert was cheered by this success, and the next day set out for Nasangkalu. On the way he met two women, who told him that they were just returning from the town, where the chief had sent them to forbid any of the people to become Christians, and to order any who should disobey him to leave the town. Mr. Calvert went on his way, and found the message had produced its effect, and none of the people would even listen to him. One of the natives, however, was so convinced of the truth of the new religion that he left the town and became a servant to a Tongan near the mission-house. He profited so well by the instruction given him that he was afterward sent as a teacher to Vatoa, near Ono, and there labored faithfully and successfully, till he closed a useful life by a happy death.

Rev. Thomas Williams and his wife arrived at Lakemba in July, 1840. They remained on this circuit, which was too large for one missionary.

The islands near Lakemba were enlightened by the gospel at the same time with its spread at Ono. It was everywhere first opposed, and then triumphant over heathenism. At Oneata, about forty miles from Lakemba, a Fijian teacher labored together with two Tahitians, already mentioned, and Mr. Cross and Mr. Calvert, while at Lakemba, paid frequent visits to them. The results of these efforts began to be manifest in the increase of conversions, till the majority of the people were Christians.

Early in 1842 a new chapel was built, with great labor, and, as the missionaries thought, far too large. But just then the King of Lakemba sent a message by a heathen Oneata priest, requesting that all would *lotu*, as it was not desirable for so small an island to be divided. Many were also waiting for this permission, and forthwith the head chief, the priests, and remaining heathen of Oneata professed Christianity, and helped to finish the chapel, which was now just the right size for the whole of the inhabitants to assemble in.

In April, 1849, the new chapel was opened and filled with earnest worshippers. These Oneata people are very industrious and enterprising. Besides planting abundance of food, and manufacturing articles for tribute, they have excelled their neighbors in commerce, thus enlarging their means of communication with other parts of the group, whence they obtained various commodities which were not made among themselves. On becoming Christians, they spread diligently the knowledge of the gospel wherever they voyaged: so that in many places they were made useful.

CHAPTER VII.

ONO.

THE earnest pleadings for a missionary's visit to the native church at this island were a source of great anxiety to Mr. Calvert, who was laboring alone at Lakemba. Already he had twenty islands under his care. The voyage occupied weeks, sometimes months, even in a good canoe,—which was hard to procure. More than all this, he had a wife and child, who must be left alone and unprotected among this ferocious and savage people.

Appalled by these dangers and difficulties, Mr. Calvert faltered. Then his wife spoke with the courage of a Christian heroine. She had come to Fiji to be a helpmeet, not a hindrance, to her husband. She also had come to work for God, and she knew he would protect her and her child. Therefore she said to him, "Do you intend to go?" "How can I?" he replied. "Why not?" she calmly asked. "How can I leave you alone?" "It would be much better," replied the noble woman, "to leave me alone than to neglect so many people. If you can arrange for the work to be carried on here, you *ought* to go." It was enough. Mr. Calvert resolved to go. Fresh news from the islands made the case more urgent. At Ono, as at Vatoa, the Christian religion was progressing, but at Ono sad events had occurred. Elated by his new position, the head teacher grew careless in the performance of his duties, and finally fell into open sin. This state of things made a visit from a missionary still more desirable; and, happily, just at this time a large canoe from Tonga arrived at Lakemba. It was commanded by a brother-in-law of King George; and arrangements were easily made with him to take Mr. Calvert to Ono.

They first visited Vatoa, where they found things in a prosperous condition. The teacher had been there five weeks, laboring industriously, and with such success that Mr. Calvert found the chief could read better than his instructor.

This chief had several wives; but he selected the oldest one, the mother of his children, and was married to her by Mr. Calvert, who during his visit married twelve couples and baptized two persons. The Wesleyan Methodist Missionary Society instructed their missionaries not to admit as a member of a church, even on trial, any one who had more than one wife. They adhered strictly to this rule, and found that the difficulties involved in it yielded to the firm enforcement of right principle. Households once turbulent and noisy became peaceful and quiet. The discarded wives were provided for, and the people generally were very willing to conform to the Christian rule.

Mr. Calvert hastened on to Ono, where he found that the accounts he had heard of the wonderful work accomplished had not been exaggerated. There was cheering evidence that many had "received the Spirit" and were leading consistent Christian lives.

Many came eagerly to Mr. Calvert to be baptized and married. He baptized two hundred and thirty-three persons and married sixty-six couples. He found also several young men anxious to be educated for teachers, to go to other parts of Fiji.

With all this encouragement, Mr. Calvert found much opposition on the part of the many heathen on the island, who were angry and alarmed at the progress of the new religion. Their ill will at last grew so strong that it was feared there would be war before Mr. Calvert left the island. Among the causes of this opposition was the fact that one of the Christians, among several wives whom he discarded, put away one who was related to a heathen of great self-importance. This man regarded it as a personal insult, and took up the matter very warmly. Mr. Calvert succeeded, however, in arranging affairs so that no actual rupture occurred between the parties.

But out of an event which took place at

this time arose a war between Ono and Lakemba, involving the Christian as well as heathen inhabitants. A young girl was converted and baptized who had been betrothed to the old heathen king of Lakemba, who already had thirty wives. After her conversion she refused to become his wife: he resented her refusal, and undertook to compel her compliance with her engagement. This was the ground of a war, which was conducted with spirit and determination on both sides. The Ono people stood very firm in their adherence to the right, and their firmness encouraged Christians in other places. The cause of the true religion prospered amidst all these apparent obstacles to its progress. The king did not succeed in his purpose, and peace was, after a time, made.

During the war the Christians and the heathen had been very harmonious in Ono, but after its conclusion the old enmity of the latter to the former began to show itself in reviling and persecution. The patient endurance of this on the part of the Christians had in time its usual effect of conciliating and softening their enemies. Before long they ceased their opposition, and sought to know more of Christianity.

Not long after peace had been concluded, Mr. Waterhouse, the general superintendent of the missions, with several of the missionaries, visited Ono. The people were expecting the arrival of the ship, and awaited it at the chief town.

Mr. Waterhouse found all the chiefs seated under wide-spreading trees, waiting for them. He then addressed them in the open air, as none of the chapels would have held the people. After service he made inquiries into the war, its causes, and the manner in which it was conducted. He was led to the conclusion that the Christian party had shown remarkable forbearance and mildness in their behavior. Many of the heathen were induced to receive Christianity, to see what was the secret of the extraordinary power it had over their neighbors and friends.

This visit had been a memorable one to

this time arose a war between Ono and Lakemba, involving the Christian as well as heathen inhabitants. A young girl was converted and baptized who had been betrothed to the old heathen king of Lakemba, who already had thirty wives. After her conversion she refused to become his wife: he resented her refusal, and undertook to compel her compliance with her engagement. This was the ground of a war, which was conducted with spirit and determination on both sides. The Ono people stood very firm in their adherence to the right, and their firmness encouraged Christians in other places. The cause of the true religion prospered amidst all these apparent obstacles to its progress. The king did not succeed in his purpose, and peace was, after a time, made.

During the war the Christians and the heathen had been very harmonious in Ono, but after its conclusion the old enmity of the latter to the former began to show itself in reviling and persecution. The patient endurance of this on the part of the Christians had in time its usual effect of conciliating and softening their enemies. Before long they ceased their opposition, and sought to know more of Christianity.

Not long after peace had been concluded, Mr. Waterhouse, the general superintendent of the missions, with several of the missionaries, visited Ono. The people were expecting the arrival of the ship, and awaited it at the chief town.

Mr. Waterhouse found all the chiefs seated under wide-spreading trees, waiting for them. He then addressed them in the open air, as none of the chapels would have held the people. After service he made inquiries into the war, its causes, and the manner in which it was conducted. He was led to the conclusion that the Christian party had shown remarkable forbearance and mildness in their behavior. Many of the heathen were induced to receive Christianity, to see what was the secret of the extraordinary power it had over their neighbors and friends.

This visit had been a memorable one to

the islanders, and had increased their desire to have a missionary living among them. But the number of missionaries was too small to enable them to spare one for this distant island. They resolved, however, to send them a teacher, Silas Faone, a Tongan of zeal and piety, who had labored successfully elsewhere.

The following year—1842—Mr. Williams visited Vatoa and Ono. At Vatoa he found the little church prospering; and he thus writes from Ono:—"The people here wept for joy when they beheld me accompanied by my noble friend Silas Faone, who is to take the superintendency of our work here. The women new-matted the chapel, and the men were engaged in making us a feast. I had not been long on the island before I was informed that the people waited for me to ask a blessing on the food which they had brought and arranged neatly before my door, comprising twenty-five baked pigs, two turtles, with fish, native puddings, two hundred bunches of ripe bananas, and hundreds of yams and cocoanuts,—abundantly testifying that the people did not love in word only. Some time after they brought me a fine mat, as a present; and a bundle of native cloth, as an expression of their love, was given to their new teacher. During my stay I was fully employed amongst them."

Mr. Williams baptized nearly two hundred persons, and found a church-membership of three hundred, many of them of undoubted Christian faith and life. The change in them seemed almost miraculous, and could be explained by nothing but the power of God manifested in them.

A heathen chief from Mbau, who had set out with the purpose of going to Tonga, had lately drifted to Ono, where he stayed some weeks. Instead of being killed and eaten with his crew, in Fiji fashion, he was surprised at receiving the utmost kindness and hospitality. After having had a full opportunity of watching the Christians, he said, on his arrival at Lakemba, "I now know that Christianity is true and good. I wish to become a Christian,—which I shall do before long; and, when I do, I shall abandon all my old ways. Fijians will be in earnest when they embrace religion."

There remained an important point, upon which the effect of Christianity was yet to be seen. This was the matter of *tribute* to the chiefs. These latter were much afraid that the *lotu* would render the people independent of their claims. The time for paying tribute came. Ono was the only place of importance where the new religion prevailed universally; and upon it the eyes of all parties were anxiously fixed. The people paid their tribute cheerfully, and thus acknowledged subjection to the authority of their government. This produced an impression in favor of Christianity through all the islands.

They now had their two Tongan teachers, together with several natives. They read eagerly and intelligently the books furnished by the printing-press.

In October, 1845, Ono was again visited by a missionary, who was gladdened by tidings of a great work of good which had been going on there. One Sunday, while the service at the adjacent island of Ndoi was being conducted by Nathan Thataki, the people began to weep aloud. The preacher was much affected, and sank down, unable to proceed. A note was sent across to Ono to the head teacher, Silas, who immediately came, and again assembled the people for service; but the emotion and excitement were so great that he was not able to preach. They then prayed together, and, as in the olden time, the Holy Ghost fell upon them in great power. Silas begged the people to go with him to Ono, and they crossed over, dividing themselves into parties for the different chapels where prayer-meetings were held. The holy influence now spread on all hands. Old and young became alarmed and earnest about their souls. In a few weeks, about two hundred persons showed good signs of having been truly saved. Great was the joy of these new converts, and whole nights, as well as days, were spent in praise and prayer. Several said they should like to die soon, lest they should sin again; and many offered to go to the most dangerous parts of Fiji, to tell about the salvation which had made them so happy.

CHAPTER VIII.

REWA.

In the year 1840, that important agent, the printing-press, was removed from Lakemba to Rewa. Mr. Cargill and Mr. Jagger arrived with it in July. The work of teaching had been begun by Messrs. Cross and Hunt; but the first had now removed to Viwa, the latter to Somosomo.

The new-comers were met, on their arrival, by Christians and heathens,—the former bent on welcoming, the other on robbing them. Some of the cases containing goods were opened on board of the canoes in their passage from the vessel to the shore, and their contents stolen. One of these robberies was committed in the presence of the missionary. Two chiefs who were on board left the canoe a short distance from the proper landing-place, and went into the low bush, where they ordered a certain case to be brought to them. The missionary was then standing on it. They supposed, from its weight, that it must contain hatchets. With much toil they finally broke it open where it stood; but instead of hatchets they found only part of the printing-press. Disappointed in this, they ordered a larger and lighter box to be brought to them. The canoe was then permitted to go on its way. The king was immediately informed of this bold robbery, and was very angry. The same evening the box was returned to the owners,—showing that the king had been prompt in his action. The missionaries found in him a friend and protector of Christianity, though he was still a heathen. His brother, Ratu Nggara-ninggio,—"*Cave of a shark*,"—joined heartily with the chiefs and priests in their opposition to and persecution of the Christians.

The missionaries found a small house

ready for them, but no chapel. They held service with the little company of converts in the open air, but were often interrupted by the stones with which Ratu's party pelted them. One of the native Christians opened his dwelling for worship; but his goods were taken from him, and he was threatened with death if he persisted. Then application was made to the king for permission to build a chapel. He not only granted this, but gave them ground near the mission premises.

When Ratu heard of this, he was exceedingly angry, and vowed that he would kill any man who dared to help in building the chapel. He might have wrought much mischief in his anger; but the king and the missionaries thought it would be the part of wisdom to defer the building for the present.

Trouble soon came to them in another form. In September a violent type of influenza made its first appearance in Rewa. The people were much terrified, and very generally attributed it to the mission families, some declaring that they had brought it from England with them, while others regarded it as a punishment from the God they worshipped.

The missionaries were diligent and successful in their care and attention to the sick, thereby proving to them the sincerity of their interest in them.

In October Ratu resolved that he would put an end to the new religion at once. With two companions he waited by the river for the return of the missionaries to the mission-house. Their intention was to shoot the two hated teachers down as they crossed. After waiting for some time, they concluded not to shoot the missionaries, but to wait for the Tongans. Thus the two men of God passed safely by. The Tongans did not come; but, late at night, as the chief and his two companions passed by the place where the Christians were holding worship, they stopped and fired their muskets into the window. Again God protected his people, and no one was hurt.

Ratu did not cease his efforts to incite the people to the persecution of the Christians. A fire broke out near the mission premises, and, eager for plunder, the natives came in crowds, Ratu among them. His brother, Thokonatu, or Phillips, was more friendly to the missionaries, and protected their houses from the fire and from the rapacious people. The next attempt was to break up the congregation when at worship, by pelting them with stones; but this too failed, as no one was hurt, and no one moved until the service was over. Their dangers, which became more frequent, kept the mission families in alarm; nor were they reassured when, on the 31st, they were awakened by strange noises on the other side of the river. On running out, they saw, for the first time, the horrid sight of the dragging of human bodies, seventeen of which were just being handed out of a canoe, having been sent from Mbau as the Rewa share of two hundred and sixty persons killed in the sacking of towns belonging to Verata.

The mission station had now become the centre of a small settlement; for several Tongans had built houses near, one of which was used as a place of worship. Some few

Rewans also dared to come out from among the heathen and make their home near the missionaries, to whose teaching they gratefully listened; while others who were sick came to live across the river, that they might get the benefit of medical care. Joel Bulu, a Tongan teacher who had been brought from Lakemba to help in printing, gave the little settlement the name of Zoar. "For," said he, "at the heathen places the people are diseased, and they cannot cure them; their souls are sinful, and they cannot save them; but when they come here they get a cure for body and soul; their bodies are generally healed, and, receiving instruction, they believe in God, and their souls live thereby. Therefore this place is a true Zoar."

Early in 1840, a terrible storm visited the island, destroying much property and deluging the houses of the common people. The missionaries and their families took refuge in a single apartment of one of the mission houses, which was on a raised foundation; but the king sent to offer them a safe residence in case the mission house should fall.

Among other devastation caused by this unusually heavy storm, a yam-bed belonging to the king was much injured. He therefore ordered the yams to be dug up, and taken as a token of his love to the missionaries. This caused great surprise among his people, who remonstrated with him for taking up the yams before the time and before the offering of the first-fruits to the gods. The king, however, was resolute, saying, "The gods of Fiji are false and weak; and, as they have not prevented the earth from being washed away from my yams, I will not present these yams to them, but to the ambassadors of the true God." Yet the king was not ready to give up entirely the service of these impotent gods for that of the one true God.

Slowly, but surely, however, the little band of Christians increased in numbers and in strength. A Rewa chief at last publicly renounced his old religion to become a Christian.

About this time Captain Hudson, of the United States Exploring Expedition, called at Rewa. He was of much service to the mission, by the decided influence which he exerted on behalf of religion through his words and conduct.

On the 2d of June, 1840, overcome by her recent alarms and exhausted by her arduous duties, Mrs. Cargill died. Her fellow-laborers felt most keenly the loss of her zealous aid in their great work, and the example of her gentle piety. The energies of her life were given to this work for six years; and she died urging those around her to more earnest zeal in the missionary cause. Among the people her very lovely character had influenced their opinion of her religion in the most favorable manner; and they yet remember and speak of her with much love. She requested that her children should be taken to England to be educated. Mr. Hunt went directly to Mr. Cargill as soon as he heard of his bereavement, and urged him to come to Somo-somo; but Mr. Cargill knew that it was best to remove his motherless children from Fiji, and as soon as possible he sailed for the colonies.

Mr. Jagger was now left alone at Rewa. His circuit was large, and the management of the printing-press—from which the station was supplied with books—depended upon him. He had, however, efficient help in the Tongan teachers. As a physician he was renowned among the natives. Sometimes he had three or four sick priests under his care, who came to him for aid after their gods had failed them. Many of his patients received spiritual as well as physical healing.

A young and influential Mbau chief, named Matanambamba, had been living for some time in Rewa. His father was killed when Thakombau took Mbau and thus crushed the revolt in which he had been a leader. The young man at that time fled to Rewa, and there waited to revenge his father's death. He hated the religion which enjoins forgiveness of enemies, and heartily assisted Ratu Nggara in his persecution of the Christians. After some months he became ill, and neither Fijian treatment nor Fijian gods did him any good. Terrible dreams afflicted him, in which he thought that he was being punished by the missionaries' God for his persecution of them and his attempts to kill them. At last, greatly humbled, he came to the mission station. Mr. Jagger attended him medically, his own friends supplying him with food.

He was now under direct Christian influence, in daily attendance on family worship; and, fearing greatly lest he was going to die, his heart became softened in genuine contrition for his sins. He was told to pray for mercy. He asked to be taught suitable words; "for," said he, "great is my desire to pray to God, but I know not what words to take up."

He went to see a poor man, named Savea, who had been cured of a loathsome disease and had become a Christian. Savea said, "I was friendless, forsaken, destitute, and treated as a dog; but I fled to the servants of God, swallowed much medicine, and trusted in the Lord. When it was night, I prayed, when morning came, I prayed; and by doing this I got well."

The young chief would once have scorned to associate with one of such low rank as Savea; now he said to him, "From this time we will be friends."

Matanambamba recovered, and was led to trust in Christ for the forgiveness of his sins. He learned to read and write, and was earnest in his efforts to lead others to Christ.

Ratu Nggara was banished from Rewa for a great offence of which he had been guilty. After an absence of some time, he returned. The king was not reconciled to him; and, from Ratu's character and influence, a civil war was feared. Mr. Waterhouse was then visiting the islands; and he presented whales' teeth to the king, with an entreaty that Ratu might be forgiven.

The offering was favorably received, but the king would not consent to full forgiveness of his brother. Tanoa of Mbau made a similar application to the king, which was disregarded. The priest who bore Tanoa's message was indignant at this, and abused the king for showing more favor to the strangers from a foreign land. To this the king replied, "I know that they are come out of love to me, and that their words are true. They speak like friends, and desire good. They do not come here to tempt. They wish this land to be prospered. No evil arises from their purposes. We are enriched by the property they bring." The god in the priest answered, "It is not good. How is it that you do not accept the offering that I bring?" "Because," said the king, "the speech of the Fijians is contrary. You say it is good not to war; and then you will go to my brother and tell him that it is good to fight. If you say one thing to me, you will say quite otherwise at Mbau."

The king yielded at last to the solicitations of the Rewa chiefs and the missionaries, and was reconciled to his brother, who was much more kindly disposed towards the missionaries in consequence of their efforts in his behalf.

Eighteen adults and six children were, in

the autumn of this year, baptized, and the spread of true spiritual religion was most manifest and cheering. The schools also prospered, and the diligence of the scholars increased as the supply of books became larger.

A Tongan, whose life had been spent in Fiji, where he had grown up a heathen, in the closest intimacy with the chiefs and people of Rewa, became truly converted, and received at baptism the name of Job. He soon learned to read and write, and was zealous in trying to do good. He had frequent opportunities of talking with large parties at the king's house. One day, in order to bring about a conversation, the king complained about Job's planting, saying that there was no need for Christian people to do that. Job, in contending for the necessity of industry, referred to the Bible. "Oh!" said the king, "how should you know any thing about books? You have never come from Tonga or England, but have dwelt in Fiji all your life." "That's true," rejoined Job; "but I can read a little, and thus I know something. Other chiefs said, "It's a strange thing that when a man joins the *lotu* he becomes wise quickly, and contends that the *lotu* is *quite* true, and Jehovah the only God. How is it?" The king said, "They read, and thus know; or else they ask the missionaries." "But how is it that they do not fear us?" asked one of the chiefs. "Oh," replied the king, "they do not fear to die; they give themselves up to their God; and life or death is good to them. But this is not the case with us. When we are sick, we ask where we shall go that we may live. We then run to one place and to another, that we may get strong. But these *lotu* people act otherwise."

On another occasion the king said, with great emphasis, "The *lotu* makes all our land to move!"

The king was right. That gospel which had "turned the world upside down had come hither also," and already its power was felt. It was no small victory gained when that mission church numbered its few first converts. They needed sincerity and firmness to enable them to come out from all that they had ever deemed most sacred and binding, and which their fellow-countrymen still regarded as such. Every form of opposition, from derision to the harshest persecution, withstood these early confessors; but they kept firm, and when others saw that these, who had been men of blood and lust and lawlessness, had become men of peace and purity, and remained so, they greatly wondered.

A mission station which had been established at Kandavu—an island under the power of Rewa—with an encouraging prospect of success, had to be abandoned at this time, Ratu Nggara having warned the Christian teachers to leave the place if they cared for their lives.

Other discouragements tried the soul of the solitary missionary in Rewa. Bodies were frequently brought opposite the mission premises, and cooked and eaten with fiendish rejoicings. A Christian woman was killed while fishing, to feast the people employed in building the king's house; and only the courage and prompt action of Mr. Jagger rescued the body from this sacrilege.

At Suva also things had lost their cheering aspect. The town was engaged in continual war with the Rewans. The teacher feared to remain, as the town was in constant danger of being burnt,—which catastrophe came at last, in 1843, when about one hundred persons were killed, and most of them eaten.

At the mission house there was family sorrow in addition to the trouble caused by these events. Two of the missionary's children had died, and he himself had a very severe attack of illness. On his recovery, much time had to be given to the re-thatching of the house. The workmen employed were idle, incompetent, and arrant thieves. Thus, the work was badly done, and, in spite of the utmost vigilance, many things were stolen. Under the weight of hindrances and trials such as these, and in the presence of scenes, none the less horrible because familiar, which cannot be described, the missionaries and teachers labored diligently on.

A few held steadfastly to their faith, and in the darkness signs of the dawn were seen by the "patient, toiling watchers." They trusted in God, and were not cast down, believing that the gospel would yet prevail in Fiji if they worked and waited long enough. The printing-press was not idle in these days of discouragement; and, a fresh supply of types and paper having been sent from England, it was not long before books were published in four of the Fijian dialects.

CHAPTER IX.

PROGRESS IN LAKEMBA.

In 1842 Mr. Williams arrived at Lakemba, and very soon built himself a comfortable house. The missionaries heretofore had trusted to the natives for dwellings, and therefore generally had uncomfortable houses, ill adapted to the convenience or health of English families. They soon followed Mr. Williams's example, and, as they were able to do so built houses for themselves.

When the mission house at Viwa was built, it consisted of two stories and an attic. None of the others had built so high; and the chiefs from Mbau came to see it. They gazed with wonder and admiration at the flat ceiling and the even walls, and broke into exclamations of delight.

In 1843 Mr. Williams removed to Somosomo, and Mr. Calvert was again alone. He began now to suffer much embarrassment from two different parties of foreigners on the island,—the Papists, who were trying to establish a mission there, and the Tongans, whose indolence made them poor, while their pride and influence caused them to be hated and feared.

The Protestants had a decided advantage over the Papists, in the influence of their domestic life and the presence and spirit of their wives. The people were, as a general thing, much attached to the Protestant families, and almost as universally they disliked the priests.

The principal difficulty the missionaries had to encounter with the Tongans was their extreme idleness, which led them into various disorderly practices. They would not work, they must live, and they were content to depend on the Fijians. The missionaries therefore directed their efforts specially to this one point,—to teach them honest industry, by precept and by practice. These efforts were not unsuccessful; for soon a somewhat better state of things began to manifest itself. The Tongans are a bold, intelligent, and powerful race, who exert much influence; and they must always be either an important assistance or a great hindrance to the labors of the missionaries. They are still a source of perplexity and trouble to the church, although many of them have commended true religion to all around them by word and deed.

In 1844, Mr. Lyth was appointed to assist Mr. Calvert at Lakemba. The church now numbered nine hundred and sixty-three members. The medical skill of Mr. Lyth was in constant demand, and this alone kept him very busy. Soon after his arrival, Toki, the inveterate hater and opposer of Christianity, died suddenly. By his death a great obstacle to the progress of religion in Lakemba was removed. Both here and in the surrounding islands a new spirit seemed to be awakened. The people were apparently moved by a sincere conviction of their sinfulness and trust in Jesus Christ.

Among a number who had been merely nominal Christians, and who now became really changed, was Jane, the daughter of King Tui Nayau, and the wife of a chief of high rank. When she became a true believer in Jesus, her heart was touched with deep anxiety for her friends. Immediately she went to the king her father, and found several persons with him. Sitting down by his side, and leaning against him, she said, "Sire, I have come to beg of you to abandon heathenism and embrace Christianity. Heathenism is false and useless; religion is good, and a very great matter. I *now know* that religion is good. The Lord has worked mightily in my soul. I now know the excellency of religion; and I have therefore come to beseech you to turn from falsehood to truth." She wept much. The king said, "Have you only now found that religion is good?" She replied, "I have only known well about religion a few days. The Lord has changed my heart. Had I known before, I should have come to you. On finding the power, I felt great love to you; and I have now come before you to beg you at once to decide." He said, "You are right and true. Most of our relatives are on your side. I shall wait a little longer, and then decide. I build no temples. I do not attend to heathen worship. There are only a few of us remaining heathens."

Lakemba was at this time threatened with war from Mbau. In former days the excited people would have flocked to the temples with offerings to consult the priests. Now the temples were deserted, and no priests were to be seen. The town was fortified, and many began to discuss the question whether it would not be better for all to become Christians at once.

The deepest anxiety was felt by the missionaries' families; for to gain the mass of the people, even as nominal Christians, was to throw a heavy weight on the right side of the scale. Tui Nayau at last announced, on Friday, January 9, 1846, that the following Sabbath he would, for the first time, worship Jehovah. But the influence of many who still opposed Christianity dissuaded him from keeping his resolution.

Under the pressure of growing excitement, the Sunday following was fixed for the king's profession of Christianity, and every thing went well till the Saturday, when the counsels of heathen chiefs were strongly backed by Romish priests, who preferred Tui Nayau's remaining a heathen to his becoming a Protestant; and once more the king drew back.

Wetasau, the chief next in rank, had formerly been very obstinate in his resistance to the truth; but now his mind was changed, and nothing could longer deter him from

In this year the mission lost one of its best native preachers,—a Tongan, named Julius Naulivou. He was a man of high rank and great influence. He had been adopted, when quite young, by a former king of Lakemba, but after he grew up he returned to Tonga, where he was converted, and then he went back to Lakemba that he might preach the gospel to his companions there. He died in perfect trust in Christ, and with words of joyful praise upon his lips. He had a friend named Wangki-i-chalani, for whose conversion he had long and earnestly prayed. Under the influence of his peaceful death, Wangki and several others forsook heathenism for the service of God.

In 1848, a large chapel was built on Nasangkalu, the third town in importance on Lakemba. Wangki here used all his influence to persuade the people to *lotu*. The teacher at this place had been a notorious robber, but was now not only honest, but willing to suffer loss and endure outrage.

Among the Levuka people—a sailor tribe

subject to Mbau—was a chief who was a notorious leader in every bold enterprise or daring robbery. His hatred of the Tongans and Christians was intense, and was manifested in active efforts to put down the *lotu* and harass the Tongans.

One evening Mr. Calvert improved a favorable opportunity to explain fully to him the doctrines of religion and urge upon him its truth and its claims. The next night the Levukan came again; and, as he listened and inquired, his conscience was troubled and his heart subdued, until the enemy of Christianity became its obedient and earnest advocate. In proportion to his former hate was his present love. He had formerly gone through Fiji, carrying outrage and distress; now he reconciled enemies, and taught that man should love his neighbor as himself. When the people wondered at the change in his conduct, he told them of the change in his heart. He built, at his own expense, a chapel for the people in his own town, and made it the most beautiful in the district.

But the usual difficulty in such cases remained with him. One thing he could not, for some time, bring himself to do. He had many wives, valuable to him for the wealth and position which they gave him. The struggle to give them up was long; but in the end the right conquered. The day when his new chapel was opened for the worship of God, he put away his many wives, and was married to one. The effect of this step, as a proof of his sincerity, and as an example to other chiefs and people, can hardly be appreciated.

In May, 1848, Mr. Calvert left Lakemba for Viwa. Lakemba was his first station. Others had at intervals labored there with him, but he had spent ten years in steady toil on this island, and whatever changes had taken place in these ten years had been mainly through his instrumentality. His attachment to Lakemba was most fervent, and his prayers for her temporal and spiritual prosperity most earnest. Mr. Malvern remained there, and was joined by Mr. Watsford and his wife. These all labored faithfully, and the good work progressed in their hands.

In 1849, Mrs. Watsford, whose health had long been failing, but who was most reluctant to take her husband from his labors, became so much worse that they were obliged to leave Fiji immediately.

Tui Nayau was much attached to Mr. Watsford; and the morning he left he presented to him a necklace of whale's teeth, and, kissing him, promised him he very soon would *lotu*. New circumstances now occurred to induce Tui Nayau to take this step. Lakemba was threatened with war from Mbau, and soon reports came of a large army on its way to attack the island. The week after Mr. Watsford left, Tui Nayau made a public profession of his faith in Christianity, in which he was joined by the only remaining heathen priest and some of his friends.

On hearing of this, the chief of the great town of Nasangkalu ordered the drum to be beaten for service, and together with many of his people joined, for the first time, in the worship of God. The following Sabbath was a day of great rejoicing on Lakemba and the other islands whither the news had travelled. Every opposition to the whole people becoming Christian was now removed.

CHAPTER X.

ONO CONVERTED.

The church at Ono now demanded the constant supervision of a missionary. Accordingly, it was decided, in 1846, that Mr. Watsford should remain there at least a year. He labored diligently with the church and the schools, and also endeavored to introduce improved methods of work among the people. This he found very difficult, as their prejudices were in favor of their old ways. He succeeded, however, in showing them how to manufacture their sinnet more easily and more economically, and contrived a machine to assist them in rope-making. He showed them how to boil down their sugar-cane, and taught them the use of arrow-root for the young and sick. He thus improved their temporal condition, and rendered himself acceptable and useful to them as a physician.

Mr. Watsford and his family suffered many privations from the delay in the arrival of supplies. One of the trials incident to the climate is thus described in a letter to some of Mr. Watsford's co-laborers on the islands:—
"There cannot possibly be any place in the world, I should think, as bad as Ono for mosquitos. I thought Rewa was bad enough; but it is nothing to Ono. No rest day or night. I cannot tell you how we have been tormented. When your letters came, we did not know what to do to get them read. We could not sit down to it. We had to walk, one with the candle and one reading, and both thrashing at them with all our might. We could not sit to get our food. And, although we did every thing we could to keep them out of the curtains, yet they

get in in numbers, and night after night we can get no sleep. Mrs. W. was wearied out, and James was bitten most fearfully. Very many of the people went to sleep at Manā, an island free from mosquitos, on the reef; and they advised us to go there, which we did at last. We had a house taken there, and lived there three weeks. We then came back to Ono. Since then we have had hot weather and fewer mosquitos; but lately we have had much rain, and they are now very troublesome. I am scratching and kicking with all my might while I write this. They never tire nor stop to rest."

In 1847 Mr. Watsford was removed, and no new appointment was made for Ono until the following year, when Rev. David Hazlewood was appointed for this important station. He was most favorably impressed by the external appearance of the Christian people, and by the great difference between them and the heathen. He had brought with him sixty copies of the New Testament in the Fijian language, as the share belonging to the place. They were to be bound;

and book-binding was a new business to the missionary. His brethren more experienced in the business had given him some little instruction; but he found folding and stitching rather awkward work. Soon some of the native preachers offered their aid, and after a little teaching they put the books together in a style which he says librarians might laugh at, but which was greatly admired and appreciated by the natives, who eagerly bought them, paying for them chiefly in sinnet.

In January, Mr. Hazlewood removed his family to a small island on the barrier reef, a mile or two from Ono, in order to escape the intolerable torments inflicted by the mosquitos. Here they remained several months, comparatively comfortable, but at great inconvenience to Mr. Hazlewood, who was obliged to cross every day in a canoe, thus exposing himself to danger and losing much valuable time.

He was, on one occasion during these months, subjected to great anxiety and distress on account of the residence of his family on the reef. He, with one of his little girls, was at Ono, his wife and two other children on the small reef-island. For several days the wind had been strong, but this day it increased to a violent hurricane. Mr. Hazlewood was obliged to stay at Ono. Through the night the roaring sea, the howling wind, and the pouring rain combined to make a most terrific tempest, so that Mr. Hazlewood and one of the teachers sat up to watch, lest the shaking house should fall. So great was the tumult without, that they did not hear the crash of a house which fell but a few yards from them. Through this long tempestuous night Mr. Hazlewood listened to the howling hurricane, and thought of his wife and children, separated from him by the foaming sea, on the little reef where any of the huge billows lashing the shores might sweep them away into the wild abyss. But he trusted in Him who ruled the winds and the waves, and doubted not that his treasures were safe in his hands. When morning came, he went out and looked towards the little island. The ruin and desolation caused by the storm were to be seen on every side of Ono; but little could be discerned on the reef. The trees were still erect, although no house could be distinctly seen standing. At noon some of the natives ventured over the still tossing sea, and in the evening returned with the glad news that all the family were safe. Their house had fallen; but they had first fled to a small building which they had propped up for the night, and when, in the morning, the waves came dashing up into it, they escaped farther from the shore, where they built a temporary shed. The men who went over had carried the small house in which they first took refuge to a safer position, and the family were sheltered therein. It was not until the third day after the storm that Mr. Hazlewood could cross to his family; and even then the passage was dangerous.

Mr. Hazelwood's stay in Ono was limited to one year; and, accordingly, at the end of that time he was removed to another station. As the need of instruction on other islands was now greater than in this one, it was thought inexpedient to station another missionary there. A Tongan teacher of deep piety and earnest zeal—Joel Bulu—was sent to take the place of the missionary; and he proved his worth so well that he was afterwards ordained. After he had remained at Ono for some time, other efficient teachers, trained by Mr. Lyth, succeeded him; and Ono is now a thoroughly Christian island. The missionary work has nowhere yet been so speedily and permanently successful as in this island. Fifty teachers have been raised up from among the natives, some of whom have gone to the distant heathen parts of Fiji, while others are still laboring at home.

We may here note a needed and most valuable addition to the mission force, in the shape of a *mission ship*, "THE TRITON," sent to the island in 1840. In it the missionaries and their native assistants made voyages from island to island, carrying supplies for living and laboring where otherwise they would not be able to remain.

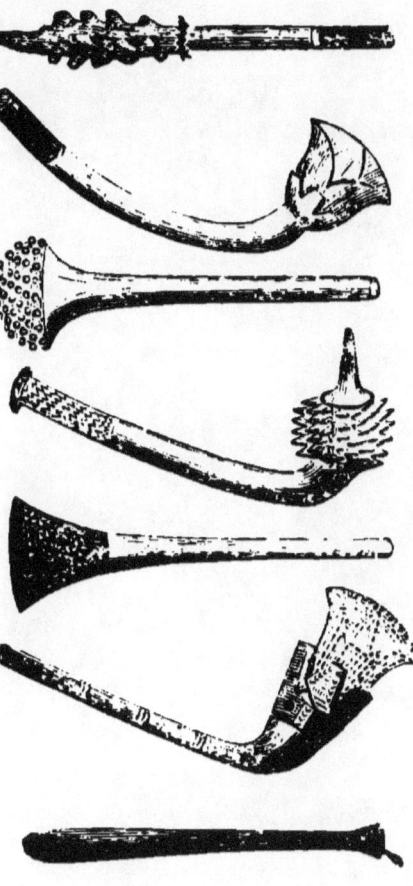

Fijian Clubs.

Page 283.

CHAPTER XI.

REWA AND SOMO-SOMO.

DARK DAYS IN REWA.

In 1843 the aspect of affairs on Rewa began to undergo important changes, which not only affected Rewa itself, but also influenced in a painful degree the mission. A quarrel had been for some time gathering between Rewa and Mbau. Thakombau was the actual head of the government at Mbau, as his father, Tanoa, was old and infirm. The smouldering fire now broke forth in the flames of war, and the conflict was waged with great fury on both sides.

The terrible sights and sounds of savage warfare for seven months continually surrounded the mission house where Mr. Jagger toiled alone. During this time, to work at the printing-press was almost all that he could do; but he rejoiced that while he was cut off from active labor at his own station he could supply the truth in printed form to other islands which were at peace.

Some foreigners who lived near the mission station sought a safer position, and strongly urged Mr. Jagger to do the same; but, having the printing-press under his charge, he determined to stay, unless the risk of doing so became greater than it then was. He speaks in writing of the astonishment which his calmness excited in both Christians and heathen, and adds, simply, "We trusted in our God." Only those who have this trust can know the "quietness and assurance" which it bestows.

In 1844, during the month of August, the whole mission family went to Viwa to attend the district meeting. The question as to the propriety of remaining at Rewa was fully discussed. All were rejoiced in seeing the family alive and well, but wondered at their brother's firmness in resolving to continue in so dangerous a position. There was no probability of an end to the war for some time, and the destruction of Rewa and its people had been declared as the set purpose of Mbau. The roof of the mission house was also in a rotten state. In peace it had been difficult to get the thatching done; now it was impossible. Food was scarce, and becoming much more so. The Rewa chiefs still clung to their gods, and still attended to the priests, though proved to be false, several of them having been killed after boastfully promising immediate victory. The king had also sent a request that there should be no more singing at the Christian worship, lest his gods should be offended.

Under all these circumstances, the district meeting resolved that the Rewa mission should for the present be abandoned, and the "Triton" was sent to effect the removal of the property to Viwa as quickly as possible. Presents were given to the king and his brother to secure their permission, and the goods were removed successfully and without loss. Two teachers, who were willing to remain, were left in charge of the small band of Christians.

After this the war continued between Rewa and Mbau, until by treachery the Mbau people under Thakombau gained access to the town of Rewa, destroyed the place, killed three or four hundred people,—among whom were ten Christians,—and made the late king's brother Phillips, according to his English name, an adherent of their own king. Ratu Nggara was a fugitive in the mountains. There he bent his energies to the collection of a force which would make him a match for Thakombau. As soon as he was strong enough, he attempted to take a town near where Rewa had stood, and was successful. There he gathered his people together, and, putting up a fence and a few temporary huts, began to rebuild the town. He sent the missionaries a message while he was doing this, telling them that the people attributed many of their misfortunes to their rejection of the gospel.

In 1847 the Mbau people again attacked Rewa, burned it, and again Ratu Nggara escaped. Then Rewa was rebuilt by the conquerors, and Phillips appointed king.

The people, though obedient to the king thus placed over them, were in favor of Ratu Nggara; and in 1851 he entered Rewa, declared himself king, and was recognized by the people.

The many attacks made by Phillips and the Mbau chiefs on him were unsuccessful. He seemed to be firmly established; and, as he had received large stores of ammunition from foreign vessels, he was fully prepared to defy his enemies.

In 1852 a native teacher was sent to watch over the mission till the missionaries could safely return. During the war, the Romish priests had sent one of their number to Rewa, who had tried diligently to get a pledge from the new king that he would forbid the return of the Protestant missionaries. This priest was much troubled by the arrival of the teacher, and begged the king to send him away. Ratu Nggara said he was afraid to do so, as the teacher had been brought by an Englishman in a British ship-of-war. This, however, was not the case, as he had been sent in the mission boat. The king was evidently glad to see him, and had now learned to value the presence and teaching of the missionary, whom he wished to bring back once more. He said he had been to the Romish service, and had learned nothing, as they did not worship in a language he understood; but from the teacher, though only a native of Fiji, he had received instruction, as he understood the language in which the service was conducted. It was evident that he thought the priest might prove useful, as he had already received presents of muskets from him, and therefore, to avoid offence, pleaded fear as an excuse for keeping the teacher.

The priests then appealed to Sir Everard Home, of her Majesty's ship "Calliope," in two long letters, complaining of the missionaries, and desiring their removal. Sir Everard, on a visit to Rewa during the war, had been impressed by the indifference of the priests to the bloodshed and cannibalism around them, and he answered in a manner most favorable to the missionaries —

speaking in the highest terms of their individual character and of the effects of their teaching, and declining to interfere in any way with their influence or instructions. About this time the chief Phillips died, and, in consequence, Ratu Nggara was joined by many chiefs and towns. Thakombau was, by a series of losses and misfortunes, much weakened, while the power of Ratu Nggara was confirmed and increased. This war continued unto the year 1852, and through these years was a constant obstacle to the spread of the gospel of peace.

SOMO-SOMO ABANDONED.

There was no station on the Fijian islands where the toil and the danger were greater, and where there was less evidence of success, than at Somo-somo. The king was in earnest in his threat to kill any who should *lotu*. Every hindrance was opposed to the missionaries. In the beginning of 1842 they had removed from the middle of the town to a more convenient and healthy position on the sea-shore. They had built there two comfortable mission houses. They visited many of the surrounding towns and villages, and found the people willing to hear, but slow to receive the truth. The habits of many of the natives were, in some respects, changed for the better, although very little "direct and decisive fruit" rewarded the missionaries' toil.

At the district meeting held this year at Lakemba, Mr. Cross was advised to leave Fiji on account of his rapidly failing health. When he had at length reluctantly decided to go, he heard of the death of Mr. Waterhouse; and, feeling that after such a loss to the mission he could ill be spared, he resolved to stay if the arrangement could be made for him to reside with Mr. Lyth and be under his medical care. It was far easier to die in the work than, under such circumstances, to leave it. Accordingly, in September Mr. Cross joined Mr. Lyth at Somosomo, and Mr. Hunt went to Viwa to supply his place.

The fatigue of moving in his exhausted condition overcame the invalid, and, notwithstanding the attention and care Mr. Lyth bestowed on him, he died October 15, 1842. He had been a missionary in the South-Sea Islands for fifteen years, seven of which had been spent in Fiji; and now he joyfully went to his rest, trusting in the Saviour whom he had loved and served on earth.

For two years longer the missionaries labored against difficulty and discouragement. Wars were unceasing, the king still resisted the claims of Christianity, and the people became constantly more indifferent. In 1847 the district meeting decided that it was not best to continue toiling on this barren ground while laborers were so much needed in other and more productive parts of Fiji. When this decision was finally reached, the greatest care had to be taken to hide the fact from the natives. For some months the missionaries were quietly at work preparing to go. They managed to get away some boxes of clothes and articles of barter, and almost all their books and other goods were packed ready to put on board the "Triton" when she should arrive.

Most of the screws were taken out of the hinges of doors and windows, so that every thing could be removed on the shortest notice.

While all this was going on, the "Triton" anchored off Somo-somo quite late on the evening of the 28th of September. Two of the brethren—Messrs. Lyth and Calvert—who had come from Lakemba to help in the removal, went ashore at once, giving orders for the boats to be at the beach early the next morning. At daybreak, the native servants, a few Tongans, and two or three Viwa people assisted the sailors in carrying the baggage to the boats, which was done very quickly and quietly. The fact that the premises were a little way out of the town helped to keep the removal more secret.

After the boats had safely deposited the most valuable articles on board the ship, the missionaries went to the king, and told him, calmly, that as he was engaged in war, and not disposed to attend to their teaching, and as the mission families had suffered very much from sickness, they had determined to leave Somo-somo for a time, and dwell in some other part of Fiji, where the people were anxious to become Christians. Having thus taken formal leave, they got all available help to forward the removal of their goods, so that when the young men returned in the evening from the fields, and crowded about the premises, there was nothing of value left on shore. Some of the natives were very troublesome, and several things were purloined. "Where are you going with that door?" asked a missionary of a man who was hurrying off with a large door. "I'm taking it down to the boat, sir." "Well, but you are taking it the wrong way for the boat: you must turn this way." And so he did; but a good many things went the wrong way before all was done. Yet far less was lost than had been expected. Towards evening a tiresome old chief took up a board, and Mr. Williams stopped him; whereat the old fellow was very angry, and seized his great club, vowing that he would kill the missionary. Mr. Calvert interposed, and begged the old chief to be quiet, and comfort himself by taking off the board; but the ship's crew were much alarmed, and seemed glad to get on board with their charge. That night all the mission party slept on board, and the next morning the "Triton" left Somo-somo.

Since the abandonment of this station, the seed so tearfully sown by the missionaries has sprung up marvellously. Civil war has desolated the island; the chiefs and people have become humbled, have regretfully remembered the kind, faithful, earnest servants of God who sought to lead them to a better life, and have greatly desired to have a teacher again sent to them. As yet, from want of means, this desire has not been gratified. The spreading of the mission work widely into other parts of Fiji has absorbed all the available men and means,—and Somo-somo waits for some one to teach its people the way to heaven.

CHAPTER XII.

VERANI OF VIWA CONVERTED.

The mission band on Viwa were at this time greatly encouraged by the conversion of their former enemy, Verani. For some time he had been satisfied that Christianity was true, but was kept from avowing his belief by a wish to help the Mbau chief in war. The more, however, he became persuaded of the importance of the truths he had heard, the more his uneasiness increased, until he always went forth in dread, fearing lest he should fall in battle and be lost forever. He still professed to be heathen, but often stole into the woods alone to pray to the one true God; and even on the battlefield he would fall down and call upon the Lord his maker.

His conviction of the claims of the Christian religion upon him steadily increased:

he made constant inquiries of the missionaries on the subject, and manifested in many ways that the Spirit was striving with his heart. He requested permission of the Mbau chief, Thakombau, to profess Christianity, but was persuaded by him to delay that step. His anxiety about his soul, and his interest in things pertaining to its salvation, never ceased. At length, at a morning prayer-meeting, with the humility of a little child, the once terrible Verani bent his knee before the one true God, and renounced heathenism with all its practices.

Not long afterwards an aggravated insult was offered to him, in the murder of a chief whose head wife was Verani's sister; but the arm once so quick to strike in bloody revenge now was unmoved. The man so jealous and so furious in his wrath was now another man; and when his own widowed sister and the other wives of the slain gathered around Verani and wildly urged him to strangle them, he stood firm, and said, calmly, "If you had come some time since, I would readily have done it; but I have now *lotued*, and the work of death is over."

Hearing of Verani's intention to *lotu*, Thakombau, when too late, sent a messenger, requesting further delay, that they might all become Christian together. The answer was, "Tell Thakombau that I have waited very long at his request; and now that I have become Christian, I shall be glad to go anywhere with my people to attend to his lawful work; but I fear Almighty God and dread falling into hell-fire, and dare no longer delay." Message after message was sent; but in vain. Verani was told that the hitherto ample supplies which he had received from Mbau would be stopped, and that he would come to be a poor and despised man. But he had counted the cost, and was not to be moved.

Verani, of his own accord, at once determined to marry one wife and put the others away. Some men of rank, whose judgment in former days he was wont to regard, pressed him to keep some of his wives as servants. But they spoke to a man whose whole heart was set against evil too fully to allow him to keep temptation, under any form, in his way. "You," said he to these counsellors, "are on the devil's side. If my wife cannot manage in our house, I will help her to get wood and cook our food; but I will not continue to sin against God."

The missionaries speak of his repentance as being proportionate to his great wickedness. His outrages and crimes had been enormous in kind and in number, and his grief became agony when the thought of the love of Christ and of his sins against that love. When he found peace and forgiveness, he longed to tell every one he knew of the Saviour whom he loved and worshipped with his whole soul.

He was baptized, choosing the name of Elijah, was married to his chief wife, and built a large new house, which he called Cherith, in remembrance of the brook beyond Jordan, where the prophet whose name he had taken was fed by the ravens.

His wife made him a happy home. He loved her very much, and found great pleasure in the progress his daughter was making at the school. Nor was family prayer neglected in this household.

Elijah Verani, as he was now called, was a man of prayer and constant communion with God.

When he was on a visit to Mbau, Mr. Williams wrote down one of his simple, heartfelt prayers as he uttered it. We give this prayer; and truly a miracle it is that a heathen so vile should thus learn the language of God's kingdom:—

"O Lord our Lord! O God our Father, whose abode is heaven! we worship before thee. We offer not ourselves, or our own righteousness, to gain thy notice: we present Jesus; we come with this our worship in his name. Thou art God; we know thee to be God. We come to thee whom once we knew not. In those days we served gods which are not gods; we were wearied in attending on them.

"O Lord the true God, have mercy on us! We are now engaged in worshipping thee; but this will not profit us if thou art away. Hear our cry, O Lord, and be with us, and help us. We are moving towards thee; do thou move towards us, and give us a blessing in this worship.

"O Jehovah, hear us for his sake, thy Son, whom thou didst give that through him we also might become thy children. Oh, hear our prayer, that the wicked may consider, and that the impenitent may become penitent and come to Christ and be saved. We would enter where Christ has entered, and be with thee. O Holy Ghost, descend upon us, and prepare our hearts for that place.

"And be with every congregation, wherever worshipping, to help them, that they may worship thee aright. O Lord, hear our cry, and be nigh unto thy work: it is thy work we have to do; but we cannot do it if thou art not near to help us. And love thy people who are bowed before thee: bless the chiefs, and the ladies, and the aged, and the children; bless them, and may they be saved.

"And bless the Christians at Lakemba, and Kandavu, and Nandi; and be with

Lazarus and those at Ndama; and be with those who live here. Bless Ra Hezekiah, and give him thy Spirit, and teach him in his goings, and help him to cast away the old strength in which he used to trust, and to trust in thy strength only,—the strength which we never knew until we heard the name of Jesus.

"And, O Lord, bless thy people in Viwa; and if one is sent to-day to preach thy gospel in Mbau, go thou with him, that the words of his mouth may be of use to the chiefs of Mbau.

"And we pray thee for our ministers: they see much evil by living with us in Fiji, and they suffer and are weak in their bodies, and there is nothing with us that we can give them to strengthen them. This only we can do, we can pray for them. O Lord Jesus Christ, hear our prayers for them. Mr. Williams is weak: do thou strengthen him, and let his life be long, and make our land good for him; and bless the lady and the children, and let thy Spirit be always with them to comfort their minds.

"These are our prayers. Oh, hear them; do thou hear them for Jesus' sake. Oh, hear them for Fiji's sake! Do have love for Fiji. When our minds think of Fiji, they are greatly pained; for the men and women of Fiji are thy people, and these thy people are strangled and clubbed and destroyed. Oh, have compassion on Fiji; and spare thy servants for the sake of Fiji, that they may preach thy true word to the people. And, O Holy Spirit, give light to the dark-hearted and give them repentance. And set us in motion, that we may not be so useless as we have been, but that we may now, and for the time to come, live to extend thy kingdom, that it may reach all Fiji, for the sake of Jesus Christ, the accepted offering for us. Amen."

Verani travelled much in different directions to spread the knowledge of the gospel wherever he could, and was a most valuable and indefatigable assistant in the missionary work. Love to God and love to man occupied his whole soul and shone in every action of his life.

Perhaps there was no man in Fiji whose conversion to Christianity was so remarkable and influential. He was so well known as a furious slayer of all who stood in his way, that the people could hardly understand the change in his character.

At the same time that there was a deep religious feeling in the Church at Ono, God greatly blessed his work in Viwa also. A revival visited the island, and, while those already Christians were awakened to greater earnestness, many hitherto careless were most powerfully and deeply moved. Their penitence for sin was proportionate to the enormity and number of what they now saw to have been the transgressions of their past lives; and in many cases the sincerity of their repentance was proved by their subsequent devotion to the service of God. The increase in church-membership resulting from this revival was two hundred, and the effects produced by it were marked in the community.

In 1848 the mission band suffered a great affliction and loss in the death of John

Hunt, who was one of the most valuable, laborious, and beloved missionaries. When he became evidently very ill, his fellow-laborers, who clung to him with a love that was mingled with reverent admiration, were deeply distressed. The natives who were his spiritual children were overwhelmed with sorrow.

So great a calamity as the loss of their beloved pastor filled the Viwan Christians with dismay, and, with one heart of grief, they gathered about that throne of grace to which his faithful hand had led them, and prayed without ceasing that his life might be spared. With mighty pleading did Verani lift up his voice among those sorrowing ones. Deeply did he love the sick missionary; and now he prayed, "O Lord, we know we are very bad; but spare thy servant! If *one* must die, take *me! Take ten of us!* But spare thy servant to preach Christ to the people!"

The unremitting care of Mr. Lyth was a source of great relief to the sufferer. While some prayed at his bedside, he wept, and became more deeply moved after they had risen from their knees, until his full heart burst forth in the cry, "Lord, bless Fiji! save Fiji! Thou knowest my soul has loved Fiji; my heart has travailed in pain for Fiji!" Those who stood by, fearing for his weak frame, tried to calm his emotion by telling him that God was blessing Fiji, and that now he must be silent. For a time he yielded, and wept low; but that great flame of devoted love must leap up in all its glory of earnestness ere it go out; and, grasping Mr. Calvert with one hand, he raised the other, crying, "Oh, let me pray once more for Fiji! Lord, for Christ's sake, bless Fiji! Save Fiji! Save thy servants! Save thy people! Save the heathen in Fiji!" That good heart was as true and mighty as ever; but the flesh was weak, and he once more became calm at the request of his friends.

He died October the 4th, after an illness of two months, in the true and certain hope of a glorious resurrection, with words of joy and praise on his lips, and undisturbed peace in his heart.

CHAPTER XIII.

MBUA AND NANDI.

The town of Mbua is situated on the large island of Vanua Levu,—the "Great Land,"—at a considerable distance from Mbau, which is on the coast of Na Viti Levu,—"Great Fiji." It is an inland town, of no considerable power, but has much interest as a mission station. The chief of Mbua sent, in 1843, for a teacher to instruct a friend of his who had become a Christian. This teacher, and others afterwards sent, never received active aid from the chief; but with his indirect sanction they labored so successfully that in 1845 there were three hundred Christians in the community. The majority of these lived at Tiliva, a small village on the island, divided from the town of Mbua by a river. Here the mission house was situated. Protracted wars had impoverished the inhabitants of the region around Tiliva, had compelled them often to save themselves from famine by eating wild roots and fruits, and had engendered among them habits of indolence and listlessness.

Although the sinnet grew luxuriantly around them, they never gathered nor plaited it. They had no comforts, and were slatternly and careless in all their domestic arrangements. Yet among these people Christianity began its work in Mbua; nor was it long before it caused improvement in their mode of life. They were induced to build substantial houses instead of mere sheds, to plant gardens, make cloth, and acquire habits of industry and order. Not only was this change wrought in their temporal condition by the coming of the gospel to them, but in many cases their spiritual nature was hopefully renewed.

Just about this time Verani was married to one wife, and immediately returned his other wives to their homes. Among them was a daughter of the Mbua chief, who resented the sending back of his daughter as a personal insult, notwithstanding Verani's explanations, and began to revenge himself on those of his own people who were converts. He prohibited the profession of Christianity, and persecuted those who dared to adhere to their new faith. The people had built a very neat chapel, which Tui Mbua caused to be burned down. The flames also consumed a house of one of the teachers; but the rest of the village was saved by the exertions of the poor people. These trials and discouragements proved too much for the faith of some among the professed Christians, and they went back to heathenism; but the greater number continued firm.

When the Somo-somo station was abandoned, it was thought best that Mr. Williams should go to Tiliva.

Mr. Williams, in writing to England in November, 1847, describes the locality of the new station as very delightful, and the common people as docile, simple, and attentive.

After a longer residence in Mbua, Mr. Williams found that the people were as depraved in most respects as in Somo-somo. Infanticide was so commonly practised among them that they could hardly be persuaded that it was wrong. The missionary was not exempt from the persecution of the Christians; and the chief—Mbati Namu—declared his intention to kill Mr. Williams, take his wife as his own property, destroy the mission premises, and let his people share the spoils. Mr. Williams suffered much from distressing anxiety for the safety of himself and his family for two months,—when the persecutor fell by violence, and was eaten by his enemies.

In speaking of the horrors, murders, and cannibalism attending and following the death of this chief, Mr. Williams says, "Enlarged views of the omnipotence of redeeming love are necessary to keep the missionary to such a people from the withering influence of despair. He appears to live amongst fiends rather than men; and, when he sees them fulfilling the dictates of their corrupt passions, he finds it difficult to believe them within the reach of mercy.

"It was a great relief to turn from such scenes to the quiet and order of the Christian village,—which had just been saved from the evil purpose of the chief,—where live many proofs of God's power to save cannibal Fijians."

At the same time that the mission at Mbua was commenced by the missionaries at Viwa, one at Nandi, a town on Vanua Levu, was established. Much good was first accomplished by a native teacher, with occasional visits from a missionary. Mr. Hunt was so much encouraged by his success that he persuaded the natives to build a mission house, with a confident hope of having a missionary stationed among them. The house was built on a swampy flat, close to the salt-water river, in a thick grove of mangrove-bushes, where there was little circulation of air to allay the suffocating heat. But here the missionaries were obliged to be; for here were the people to whom they were to minister. The health of the mission families suffered but little from the disadvantages of their situation. The station was occupied in November, 1847, by two young missionaries, with their families,—Mr. Watsford, who had been for some time laboring at Viwa and Ono, and Rev. James Ford, who had just arrived from England, after a voyage of a year lacking ten days.

The newly-arrived missionaries had been but two months in Nandi when a most severe hurricane visited the island. Mr. Watsford, in his journal, gives a thrilling account of it. After many of the natives' houses had been blown down, the mission house, being stronger, still stood; but in three days the tempest returned with increased violence. Some of the teachers and people assembled at the mission house, and worked diligently to keep the rocking house from falling. The children were collected near the door, wrapped in blankets; while the parents stood ready to rush out with them as soon as the house actually began to fall. In an hour's time one side of the house fell in, the door was dashed open, and they rushed out; but the violence of the wind and rain beat them back. As soon as they could, they made their way to an out-kitchen; but constant efforts were necessary to make it safe. They had been here but a half-hour when two young men from the town came to tell them that the water was rising so rapidly that they must fly instantly or they could not escape. The peril seemed equally great whether they went out into the storm or remained where they were. They determined to leave their shelter. The children were given to the care of natives, the two ladies placed on the backs of other natives, and, with a prayer to God, they went out.

Mr. Watsford writes, "It was a fearful time as we hurried along to the town. The cocoanut-trees bent over our heads and fell around us; the nuts were flying in every direction; the rain beat like shot in our faces; and it was with the greatest difficulty we could keep on our feet, the wind being so strong. We had to wade through the water, and in many places it was up to our necks; we had to cross a part of the river where a long tree was thrown across for the bridge; the flood was very rapid, and we were in imminent danger, but, thank God, we got over. After some time, we all reached the town, and ran into one of the teachers' houses; but we soon had to leave it again, as we thought it would fall upon us. We then got into a small house which appeared stronger than the others; and, being on a raised foundation, we thought the flood could not reach us. Here we remained about an hour, shivering with cold, our clothes being soaked by the rain.

"While we were in this place, many houses fell around us, and the water continued to rise very rapidly; and now it reached the step at the door. The night was coming on, and we began to think of some plan of getting to the mountains before dark. The teachers tied a number of bamboos together for a raft, and we sent Mrs. Ford and Mrs. Watsford first: the natives swam and pushed the raft along. They had great difficulty in managing it, and we were afraid they would be thrown off; but, through the goodness of God, they were landed in safety at a house at the foot of the mountain, which was only one inch or so above the water. The raft returned, and Mr. Ford and I got on it. We had to leave our dear children behind, except my little girl, whom I carried in my arms. I had wrapped the blanket closely around her, and held her close to my breast to screen her from the storm. She cried very much for some time, and then she moaned a little, and I thought my child was dying. I felt her little face, and it was cold as marble. When, however, we reached the house, she revived again. Our other children were then brought, and the natives carried them up into the mountain and returned for us; but while they were away we found that the water had gone down a little: we waited a short time to be certain, and then sent for the children, who were brought back nearly dead. How truly thankful we were to be allowed to remain in this little shed!

"About six o'clock the storm began to abate; but we could not get near our house to get dry clothes; and if we could have got to the house we could not have obtained what we needed, as nearly all our things were, or had been, under water. I happened to have some Ono native cloth on a shelf in a native house, which the flood had not reached. This we cut up into dresses; and, taking our own clothes off, we wrapped some of it around us, and felt a little more comfortable. Our teacher cooked us some food, of which we partook; and then, having engaged in prayer, we spread some cloth on the ground and lay down to rest. What a day this has been! In all we have passed through, how great has been the goodness of God! What a mercy that it was day! Had the storm come on at night, I do not know what we could have done. Our extremity was God's opportunity."

When the storm ceased, and they succeeded in getting to their house, they found nearly all of Mr. Ford's books destroyed, and their groceries, clothes, and furniture almost ruined by being under water for hours. And more grievous than all these losses was one which fell upon Mr. Watsford a few days later, in the death of his little girl, resulting from her exposure in the terrible storm. Mrs. Watsford also became so ill that they sent to Viwa for Mr. Lyth to visit her. On his way to answer the call, he was wrecked at Ovalau, and lost some valuable books, clothes, and manuscripts.

Mr. Watsford now secured a higher and better location for the mission house. A large wooden building, with a veranda around it, was erected. A year's experience, however, proved Mr. Ford's inability to stand the climate, and he was obliged to return to England.

Mr. Watsford remained in Nandi for nearly a year, and then removed to Lakemba, and Mr. Hazlewood took his place in October of 1848. Mr. Hazlewood had been at Ono for some time past. The difference between those he had left and his new charge struck him forcibly. The people there, having been some time under the influence of Christianity, were clean, well dressed, of good complexion, and had made advancement towards civilized life. Here they appeared miserably poor, degraded, and savage.

In the towns and villages around Nandi, Christianity gradually found its way. A chief of one of these towns, with many of his people, sought instruction from the missionaries; and soon a large and good chapel was built for their use. Teachers were sent to these places, and among them to a town fifty miles distant, where there were now several Christians. Thus Mr. Hazlewood was busily occupied in ministering to his own immediate flock, visiting his teachers at other points, and fulfilling all the numerous and varied duties of a missionary. The Christians were not without persecutions from their heathen neighbors; but one by one the little company slowly increased.

CHAPTER XIV.

PROGRESS OF THE GOSPEL ON THE ISLANDS.

The word of God had now (1850) gained a firm footing on many of the Fiji Islands. In others it was making an entrance. In yet others the savage islanders had heard of the progress of the "*lotu*," and were prepared to consider the claims of the new religion brought to them by the wonderful white men.

From Lakemba, whose missionary history we have already followed, Messrs. Lyth and Malvern made progress to other islands. Here they were often cheered by finding converts where no white man had labored. Their institution for training native teachers had enabled them to send forth Fijian missionaries, whose words were heeded by their heathen countrymen. The last heathen priest on Lakemba was baptized in 1850. In the islands around there were many converts.

At Nango, Mr. Malvern in one day baptized twenty-nine adults and nineteen children, married twelve couple, preached, and administered the Lord's supper. He left Nango the next day, intending to return home; but the wind was contrary, and he was obliged to change his course. After a rough voyage he reached Nayau, an island fifty miles off. He writes:—"Soon after our arrival, I saw that it was the hand of the Lord that had brought us hither. I found the *lotu* in a better state than at any place to which I had been. Nearly the whole of the adults on the island, I should judge, are in possession of, or are earnestly seeking, salvation. One of their leaders said that twelve months ago they were like a canoe with her point unsettled,—first shifting this way, then that way, instead of sailing direct for the land she was bound for; but now they are *mua donu*,—sailing straight,—their minds fixed for serving God and getting to heaven. We here baptized more than a hundred Fijians."

At the close of 1851 the people of Lakemba were reformed outwardly, being decently clothed, and having relinquished their obscene midnight dances and songs for the pure worship of God. Their domestic condition was also greatly improved by the lessening of polygamy. Christianity gave the Fijians what they never had truly before,—*a home*. Those who had known Lakemba and its dependencies twelve years ago marvelled at the almost universal change which was brought about. Scarcely a temple was left standing, and the sacred foundations on which they were once were now cultivated as garden-plots. Club-law was utterly abolished. A fine chapel, to which the people eagerly flocked, graced every town; and not a heathen priest was left. About eight hundred children were assembled daily in the schools, and nearly two-thirds of the adult population were church-members, affording good evidence of their desire to "flee from the wrath to come," while a large and growing number gave every reason to believe that they were renewed by the Holy Ghost. During this and the previous year one thousand three hundred baptisms were registered,—eight hundred adults, none of whom received this sacrament without having brought forth fruits meet for repentance and showing a sincere desire to trust on Christ for salvation. Everywhere, too, was found a great hunger for the word of God. The mission press could supply but a small number of Testaments, and the missionaries were pained in being obliged to refuse the people, who were willing to pay well of their property, or make any sacrifice, to obtain the Scriptures.

Mr. Collis's school prospered, a growing interest manifesting itself, and eager ambition to excel in Scripture knowledge. The children were taught reading, spelling, writing, arithmetic, geography, natural history, and singing. Mrs. Collis assisted her husband in the girls' school, instructing them on religious subjects, in addition to lessons in sewing, knitting, and other feminine occupations. A class of young men held weekly was regularly attended by nearly a hundred pupils,—many of them coming six or seven miles in the worst weather to enjoy its privileges.

The Lakemba schools have been well sustained, and efficient teachers have gone forth from them to other parts of Fiji,—thus affording valuable aid to the missionaries throughout the islands.

REWA.

As this island was now comparatively tranquil after its wars and tumults, the missionaries sent word to the people that they were ready to resume their labors among them, as they had promised when they left. Ratu Nggara, the former enemy of the Christians, gladly welcomed them back, and gave a fine large house, built for the accommodation of strangers, to the missionaries.

Here they established the station, and Ratu Nggara showed every disposition to protect and befriend them.

This quiet was, however, of short duration. War with Thakombau, chief of Mbau, was soon renewed. Koroi Ruvulo, one of the Mbau chiefs, a man to whom Ratu

Nggara owed much assistance, urged him strongly to become a Christian and then carry on the war. This the king refused, saying, "If we all *lotu*, we must give up fighting,—as it will not do to pray to the same God and fight with each other."

In September a skirmish took place, in which several Rewans were killed, and their bodies taken to Mbau. Ratu Nggara was determined to be revenged on Thakombau, although he was told that the bodies were not eaten, as he had believed He sent word to the missionary at Mbau, Mr. Moore, to leave the island, as he was about to attack it with hordes of warriors. The message was not regarded by the servant of God. Ratu Nggara was resolute in his purposes of wrath, in spite of the remonstrances of the missionary and others. Thakombau sent messages of peace and acknowledgment of his own offences to the king; but he was met by contempt and anger, and the God of the Christians defied to save Mbau or its chief from his revenge.

Impatient of delay, the Rewa chief upbraided his priests with the falseness of their predictions of speedy victory. They alleged as a reason the ruinous state of several temples. The temples were accordingly rebuilt, and plentiful sacrifices offered. The beating of the *lotu*-drum was forbidden, and the Christian worship might no longer be celebrated in the usual place, lest the gods of Rewa should be made angry. The priests expressed themselves satisfied, and promised full success. Every effort in the way of religious observance and warlike preparation was being made for the overthrow of Mbau, when the principal mover in it fell sick. But in his sickness Ratu Nggara continued to harden his heart, and on the 26th of January, 1855, died of dysentery, and was buried in one of the new temples, at the building of which the priests had promised him dead bodies in abundance.

Some Rewa towns were now willing at once to turn to Mbau; but Thakombau declined the offer, being anxious to secure peace at once. He therefore sent a messenger to the Rewa chiefs, who consented to the termination of the war. But much bad and angry feeling still existed. Many were averse to peace, and Mr. Moore was suspected of having given the late king poison in his medicine. Still, the peace was formally ratified, and on the 9th of February the peace-offering was received at Mbau with beating of drums, flags flying, and every demonstration of rejoicing. At midnight Mr. Moore was awakened by the crackling of fire in the adjoining house. Mrs. Moore and the children were hurried out in their night-clothes to a small dwelling near. The people gathered in great numbers, and there was much excitement. Mr. Moore called out to them to take what goods they could get. This was well thought of; for they set eagerly to work to carry off the property, and, as was found out afterwards, were thus diverted from their object of destroying the missionary and his family. One man, it was said, lifted his club to kill Mrs. Moore, but was prevented by a Rewan. The mission family, undressed as they were, hastened off to Mbau for shelter. Having put his wife and children in safety, Mr. Moore returned at once to Rewa, where, in the midst of danger and loss, he continued to persevere in his work. A great deal of his property was consumed by the fire, and the natives had stolen the rest.

Troublous times did not now end. A new war, in which the Christian King George, of the Tongan Islands, was involved, broke out; but peace was finally established.

On their return from a victorious campaign, the Fijian and Tongan warriors as they passed up the river in forty large canoes, with streamers flying from the mast-heads, excited much notice. Occasionally they were joined by chiefs some of whom had for years been at war with each other, but now met on friendly terms in the Tongan king's canoe.

They spent the Sabbath at Rewa, and the Rewans, Mbauans, and Tongans assembled for public worship, conducted by the English missionaries (Mr. Calvert and Mr. Moore), on a spot formerly sacred to the rites of heathenism. The sight was a strange and gratifying one,—these two tribes of Mbau and Rewa, so long at war, together peaceably worshipping the living God.

The king provided liberally and kindly for Mr. Calvert and Mr. Moore.

At a feast held at Rewa during this visit, peace was solemnly established, with the following proclamation of punishment for transgressing it:—

"Any town offending by taking any steps towards war will be considered the enemy of all, and will be liable to chastisement by the combined powers of Mbau and Rewa."

During these times of tumult in Rewa, Mr. Moore had built a small house for his family, and now, in 1855, to the joy of some and the astonishment of others, he removed his family there, trusting in God for protection from savage violence.

Mr. Moore had at times been greatly discouraged when he saw the little success attending the labor expended on this mission. But the people were becoming familiar with the claims of Christianity, and, after the war was ended, seemed inclined to give attention to them. A man of rank and influence at this time publicly abandoned heathenism and professed Christianity. This made no small stir; and the chief men assembled and demanded his reasons for taking such a daring step. He replied, "I have been induced to become a Christian because our priests are false, and because the king's priest, while striking the posts, promised that he would bring the late king to life after he was dead; also because Mr. Moore's house was burnt without my being told of it, which has grieved me." The chief had well considered the step, and now remained firm, notwithstanding the efforts made to turn him from his purpose. Another consultation of chiefs was therefore held, when it was resolved that they too should *lotu*, that peace should be permanent, and that all the towns and islands belonging to Rewa should be urged to serve the one true God.

The arrival of several Christians, among them a chief from Lakemba, did much to strengthen the good work. The hearts of the laborers were rejoiced by the springing into life of the seed they had planted. Many of the people were earnestly asking for instruction; and in not a few households there was daily family prayer.

The Roman Catholics abandoned Rewa this year, discouraged by their small success.

Mr. Moore, in the following year, wrote thus to England:—

"Wide doors have been open before us all the year, but we have not been able to enter them, for the want of help. Many have been the cries, 'Come over and help us;' and many the schemes resorted to in order to get help. Some have begged, some have sent presents, some have threatened to return to heathenism, some to Popery, and others who are Papists (in profession) have promised to join us if we could send them a teacher; but in most cases we have only been able to give a passing call, and endeavor to satisfy them with a promise.

"From our last report you would learn of the vast numbers who in a few days made a profession of Christianity. We had feared that there would be a great relapsing to heathenism this year; but we are thankful to be able to report that such cases have been very few, and only where we have not been able to supply teachers. The work has been progressing all the year, our numbers having doubled those of last year." There were at this time sixteen thousand attendants on Christian worship in the Rewa circuit.

Mr. Moore, in 1857, says, "I have little time to study: go, go, go, is the order of the day. The work extends on every hand, and we want a thousand bodies to be in a thousand places at once, to do the great work of this circuit." In later years the good work continued to spread and deepen, filling the hearts of the laborers with joy and with great gratitude to God.

CHAPTER XV.

PROGRESS AT VIWA, MBUA, AND NANDI.

AFTER the death of Mr. Hunt (1849), Mr. Calvert, who had been ten years at Lakemba, was appointed to remain at Viwa with Mr. Lyth. He had frequently visited Viwa, and was well acquainted with Thakombau the noted chief of the adjacent island of Mbau, and, in common with all the missionaries, took a deep interest in him and his people.

The custom of giving presents to the chiefs and people had grown to be a burdensome tax upon the missionaries, although at first it was a matter of necessity. Mr. Calvert determined to abolish the system as it now existed, and reduce it within proper limits. Mr. Hunt's kind heart had led him so to conform to this custom that Thakombau once said, "He is ready to give when he can ill spare the article we beg. He is a kind man.

But the missionary at Lakemba gives you such a preachment and lecture when you beg of him."

When Mr. Calvert received his goods from Lakemba, Thakombau went on the vessel with him. According to usage, Mr. Calvert, as a new-comer, made him an offering of property from the district he had left. On their way to the shore, however, Thakombau was obliged to listen to a "preachment and lecture." Mr. Calvert told him that he had come from his home in England to teach the people of Fiji of the true God and of Jesus their Saviour, who could save them from their sins; that his one great object was to lead them to obtain and practise the religion of this Saviour. "I have brought medicines from England," he said, "and have gained some knowledge of diseases and their remedy, and shall have pleasure in relieving you of pain when I can, that your life may be prolonged for repentance, prayer, and the service of God. While this is the only object I have in view, I am aware that you are destitute of many articles which we have in

England, and which would increase your comfort. Some of these I can obtain for you by writing to my friends in England. I shall be glad to do so, as I should like to see you improved and raised in temporal matters. Only, when I send for goods, I have to pay for them, *and you must pay for whatever I obtain for you.* We give our time and energies for your salvation; but we have not come to supply you with worldly riches. Yet, if you will pay for what you require, we will try to obtain useful articles for you." Thakombau listened complacently, soothed by the present just given, and said he was glad to know the right plan, and should like to be informed of what was expected in payment for any articles he might hereafter desire.

This plan was henceforth steadily pursued at Viwa, and was found to be of much advantage to the people as well as to the missionaries.

The progress of Christianity at Viwa after this time was steady, though not without hindrances and drawbacks. Most of the people were nominal Christians. Na-mosi-malua continued a firm friend of the missionaries, and Verani was a devoted Christian until his death.

The missionaries extended their labors among the surrounding islands, Viwa being the central station. From here teachers were sent out, and missions supported at many neighboring islands. The political position and importance of the island have declined; but in civilization and in religion it is inferior to no other in the group.

MBUA.

Mr. Williams, in his letters of 1849, from Mbua, on the large island of Vanua Levu (not the island of Mbau, it will be noted), speaks of visits he made to several surrounding towns, in which he was accompanied by Ra Hezekiah Vunindanga, the chief of Tiliva. This man, a few years before, had been a most bitter enemy of Christianity, but was now an earnest and consistent believer.

Some of their interviews with chiefs and others were of great interest; and they almost uniformly found respect for Christianity, if not conviction of its truth. At one village Mr. Williams was taken by the chief to the temple to sleep, and a place given him near the chief. "I had," he says, "a block of wood for my pillow, and the roof of the temple for a coverlet. When Ra Mbombo [the chief] took his place, I was fixed, with scarcely elbow-room, between two veteran cannibals, who were very curious, and plied me with questions for several hours of the dark night. On the morning of the 5th we conducted a short service among our heathen bedfellows, and then set off to the canoe."

Mr. Williams was much interested in improving the architecture of the people. He therefore built a neat and substantial mission house, and a chapel superior to any thing known in Fiji. In the latter work the people gladly aided him. He says that Ra Hezekiah was of opinion that the best material and workmanship should be expended on the house of the Lord his God. Acting in accordance with this principle, he, and some of his men who had fame for "lifting up the axe," travelled over many miles of the surrounding country in search of timber for the frame of the building. Whilst they were thus employed, the old men enlivened the village by the rap, tap, tap of the beaters with which they separated the fibre from the fleshy part of the cocoanut-husk, that it might be plaited into sinnet for the ornamental lashings. At intervals of two or three days, the joyous shout of the returning wood-cutters broke the quiet of the evening,—a signal at which those who were left in the village—old men, women, and children—ran off to assist their weary friends in dragging some giant of the forest to the spot where it was to become a pillar in the Lord's house. Happier groups than these formed, eye never saw. In about three months, eighty beams of from twelve to fifty feet long were collected, many of them from a distance of ten or twelve miles, and by manual labor only. The logs were *vesi*, or green-heart, the most valuable timber in the islands. These were carefully wrought into a very substantial frame, completed by walls and roof. The interior of the church was adorned by two colonnades of sixteen mahogany pillars each, three feet apart. It was ornamented most elaborately with sinnet and highly-stained reeds.

The people cheered each other in their work by singing and chanting, different parties responding one to the other, and then joining in full chorus.

One of the heathen chiefs sent them word that they were few and doing a great work: if they wished, he would help. So a party of his people came and built one wall and one side of the roof, substantially and well.

In 1850 war commenced in the Ndama district, and Mr. Williams went thither to try to restore peace. Accompanied by the chief and five leading men, he went to the fortress where the principal movers of hostilities were assembled, to entreat them to finish the war by becoming Christians. The sun was setting as they reached the fortress. They took their seats among groups of grim-looking men covered with black powder, and stacks of muskets, clubs, and spears; and the "noon of night" had passed before they arose from those seats. There was hard pleading on both sides. The heathen thirsted for revenge: four of their party were dead, and others wounded, and they had not drawn blood from their enemies. However, at length Mbalata, their chief, yielded. He put his hand into the hand of the missionary, and said, "I should like to be a heathen a little longer; but I will *lotu*, as you so earnestly entreat me." A young warrior bowed with him, and at the silent hour of midnight, in the open air, they worshipped the one true God together. In another part of the village, twelve women, for the first time in their lives, bowed the knee to Jehovah and said "Amen" to petitions offered for their present, future, and eternal happiness.

Mr. Williams writes, "The second object of my visit—a peace betwixt Ndama and Na Sau—engaged my attention at an early hour next morning." This object was attained with less difficulty than he anticipated. In the presence of Mr. Williams and a party of Christian chiefs, the leaders of both parties, with some of their followers, met in an area enclosed by lofty trees. Upon the entrance of the Na Sau chief, Tui Mbua, the Ndama chief, arose and cordially embraced him, to the unutterable joy and relief of the Christians who were present. At the request of Mr. Williams, Tui Mbua stated, in an animated speech of some length, the object of their meeting, his own earnest desire for peace, and his intention to be a Christian from that time forth. Afterwards Ra Hezekiah Vunindanga, the Christian chief of Tiliva, addressed the people. He began by saying, "This is a good day: we have long prayed that we might see this day; now we see it, and are glad. To-day we see the great power of God. Man could not do what we see done to-day. We Fijians are a perverse people; *we* are Fijians, and we know that of all crooked, obstinate things the mind of a Fijian is most crooked and most obstinate. If we have an enemy, we do not like to be of one mind with him; we do not wish to be reconciled to him. If some Fijian chief of great power had this day come to unite us, he could not have done so; certainly not,—certainly not,—certainly not. If some great chief of Britain had come amongst us to-day to dissuade us from war and make us one, he could not have done so. The Fijian mind defies the power of man. But what do we see to-day? We see those who the other day were full of bad feeling towards each other, and shooting at each other, sitting together in peace; hatred is taken away; and we who so lately had each different views are now united, and our minds are as the mind of one man. Ask no more, 'What can the *lotu* do?' after what your eyes see this day. The *lotu* is of God; and what we now see is the work of God: he alone is almighty. In this age we see also the love of God. He has shown his love to us by giving us his book to tell us of the Saviour and to teach us the way to serve God. And, to help us to understand what we read, he has sent his ministers to our land. Great is the love of God. We Fijians are born in darkness and error, we are reared in error, it is our nature to err, so that it is important that we have those amongst us who can direct us. A father who loves his children tells them what they ought not to do, and he tells them what they ought to do. Mr. Williams is as a father to us. If we take a step without advice, it is a wrong step; but if it is approved by him we are no more double-minded, but go fearlessly on, and we find that we are doing what is right; but our own plans lead us wrong, and the end of them is pain and trouble. Great is our joy at this meeting. You, our friends of Ndama and Na Sau, have come into a good way; never go from it. Grasp firmly what you have now taken hold of: the end thereof is life,—life now, and life forever."

Thus did the gospel change the hearts and lives of the heathen and bring peace.

Mr. Williams was joined in 1852 by Mr. Moore, and together they toiled patiently and earnestly with the islanders of Vanua Levu. Dangers came from new wars, but they were kept in safety. From the climate, however, they suffered so that, in 1853, Mr. Williams was compelled to sail for Australia.

Mr. Moore remained a year longer at Mbua, on this island, when he was sent to Rewa, Mr. Malvern taking the district he left.

The congregations had now increased to two thousand regular attendants. Mr. Malvern soon added to the mission buildings a school-house. To the schools he gave great attention.

The chief Tui Mbua, after long indecision, at last, in August, 1855, made an open and sincere profession of Christianity, and his example was followed by many of his chiefs and people.

The two Christian chiefs Tui Mbua and Ra Hezekiah now labored together to promote the true religion.

Mr. Wilson, who succeeded Mr. Malvern in 1856, wrote most hopefully of the work of God at this station. He says, "The preachers are zealous and pious, the members appear sincere, and some of them are clear in their experience. At Ndama, a place which has suffered much for religion, we have a flourishing cause: the chapel is too small for the congregation. They have contributed in mats, cocoanuts, and oil, what has paid their teacher. Since I began this letter, a native preacher who volunteered to go to a great distance to a heathen population, and who left his wife and children behind him, has returned with a chief. They report that twenty-five have embraced Christianity, that many are waiting until the missionary can go, and then they will become Christians. The chief waited on me this morning, and brought a turtle-shell as his *love*, and made a speech on behalf of himself and the head-chief, which was in effect that they wished a missionary to go and live with them, and then all in Mouta would become Christians. God has given us favor in the sight of the people; and in no place in the world could money be spent more for the benefit of the human race, nor missionaries labor in a field where they could bring a larger revenue of glory to God, than in Fiji at this day. The work is marvellous and overwhelming. Surely Christians in England who have loved Fiji so long and have given so much will do yet more, and make an effort to send a reinforcement of missionaries, seeing that their Lord has honored them so highly by giving such success to their efforts.

"It fills our hearts with gratitude, and tears of joy swim in our eyes, while we see what God hath wrought. Every day schools are conducted in temples once heathen, into which if a woman or a little girl had entered a short time ago they would have been laid bleeding victims on the threshold; we walk over ovens in which men were regularly cooked, but they are filled up, and yams are growing around them; we pass by houses in which human beings were eaten, but now we hear the voice of praise and prayer; we visit the sick, and we hear them say that they are passing away to be with Jesus."

On the 12th of August, 1857, a festival for the children took place. "*A school-anniversary and missionary meeting* IN FIJI!" As many as five hundred children were present. The exercises were in the open air, and consisted of hymns sung, the chanting of Scripture, and repeating of the catechisms.

NANDI.

Whilst at other points the work was glorious, from Nandi, on the south side of the island of Vanua Levu, from year to year sad tidings came. Good men labored until, in broken health, they were laid aside or died. In 1858 the station was left vacant.

And now came war in Nandi. The heathen, resolved to destroy the new religion, made many unsuccessful efforts to accomplish their purpose. At last Tui Levuka, from Mbau, with Tuara, Thakombau's brother, came to their assistance. The Christians had hitherto succeeded in defending their towns against their foes, who finally accomplished by stratagem what they had failed to do by force. Tui Levuka and his allies anchored off the mission premises. Telling the people that they had come at the request of the missionaries to protect the town, the wily enemies were admitted; whereupon they rushed in, set fire to the town, and speedily laid it in ashes. Tui Levuka, with unusual humanity for a heathen, refused to allow the usual privilege of massacring the inhabitants; but they were subjected to insult and outrage and shared out as captives among the towns on the coast. The mission-house escaped the flames, to be broken into and rifled.

CHAPTER XVI.

DAY-DAWN IN MBAU.

THAKOMBAU, the powerful chief of the small but important island of Mbau, near the large island of Viti Levu, had steadily refused to receive a missionary. The missionaries who were brought in contact with him always took a deep interest in him, on account of his high position and his personal character. Mr. Calvert and Thakombau had always been on very friendly terms; and Mr. Calvert faithfully endeavored to awaken his conscience. When he was stationed at Viwa, Mr. Calvert anxiously desired to extend his influence to Mbau. On the visits

Island of Mbua.

Page 346.

which he frequently made to that island, he always sought an interview with the chief. Often these visits were returned, when Thakombau would seek a private interview with the missionary in his bedroom or little study and converse for hours, generally starting such objections as would bring out the strongest arguments against the heathenism of Fiji,—which arguments, on leaving, he would use in opposing his own priests and chiefs. Whatever other effect was produced upon Thakombau, it was certain that his opposition to the *lotu* was restrained; and this was no small gain.

Permission was quietly given to a few persons in Mbau to become Christians, and among these were some women of rank. The number increased until Thakombau was alarmed and forbade all public Christian worship. Tanoa, his old father, was more favorable to the Christians, and gave them leave to hold services at Sembi, a town near Mbau, where some of his own women resided. The missionaries went there regularly from Viwa on the Sabbath, and always took Mbau on the way home; so that, though they might not have public worship, they could, by appearing in their Sunday costume, at least remind the people of the religion which kept every seventh day holy.

The strict observance of the Sabbath made such an impression upon Thakombau that he ordered a feast which had been appointed for the Sabbath to be postponed till Monday.

The power of the gospel was manifestly beginning to tell on this chief. His outward respect for all Christian observances was uniform; and he frequently expressed to priests and chiefs his opinion that Christianity was "the one true thing in the world," and that it would prevail.

About this time the Mbutoni people came to Mbau, after a long absence, to pay tribute, and it was deemed necessary to entertain them with suitable honors. These honors included a cannibal feast; and for this victims must be obtained.

The missionaries were absent from Viwa; but Mrs. Calvert and Mrs. Lyth were at home, and heard ominous sounds betokening the horrible preparations for the still more horrible feast. Procuring a canoe, these heroic women went alone to Mbau, if possible to save some of the victims from this dreadful fate. With the protection of an "unseen guard" round about them, they passed unmolested through the half-maddened cannibals into the presence of the king, and begged him to stop the work of death. They then went to the chief of the fishermen, who supplied material for these feasts, and appealed to him to sacrifice no more lives. They succeeded in persuading these men to let the victims suffice who had been already killed; and even in Mbau there were some who blessed these noble women for the work done this day.

The islands were in 1849 visited by Captain Erskine, of her Majesty's ship "Havannah." This officer did all in his power to strengthen the influence of the missionaries, and particularly took occasion to express his horror at the practice of cannibalism, in an address to the chief,—Mr. Calvert interpreting. Thakombau afterwards begged Mr.

Calvert to tell Captain Erskine that the custom of eating men was one they had derived from their fathers, but that they of the present day knew better and would give it up.

Many visitors to the islands at this time noticed that the people were unwilling even to mention cannibalism, and that some of them pretended perfect ignorance of it. Captain Erskine particularly requested Thakombau to prevent any human sacrifice on the occasion of an anticipated visit from the Somo-somo people, and further entreated that when his father Tanoa should die—an event evidently not distant—he would not allow any strangling of women. The first request the chief granted, but he said he could not make any promise with regard to the second.

Thakombau was gradually yielding. When some Christians came to visit Mbau, he gave them one of his houses to worship in. They continued to meet here, although much annoyed by the people. The favorite little son of Thakombau was permitted to attend regularly, dressed in the *lotu* dress and accompanied by his train of attendants.

The missionaries now thought it time to apply to the king for ground to build a mission house at Mbau. This request was granted; and the chief and his father, to the relief and pleasure of the missionaries, announced that they would erect the buildings. It seemed at last that their long-desired object was to be attained, and that the station would be permanently established. But, before the work was begun, a long-existing war with an adjoining district was rekindled, and, in the excitement attending it, Christianity was little remembered.

Mr. Calvert, wishing to induce the king to be merciful in the coming combat, if not to avoid it altogether, spent three days with Thakombau previous to the setting forth of his army. His efforts were attended by a measure of success.

After the heathen rites the god was said to have manifested himself through the priest, and promised victory. The expedition started, certain of success; but, in spite of preconcerted treachery, they had to retreat hastily, with a priest and several others wounded. The offerings had failed, and the old system proved false,—whereby its hold on the people was loosened and fresh vantage-ground given to the teachers of the truth. There were many signs of this lessening power of the old religion. During the absence of the army on this expedition, food was frequently eaten without the customary offering to the gods; and, when he returned, Thakombau declared his intention of taking the priest to task for his false prediction. It was strange that this man, who opposed the establishment of Christianity, should reprove openly those who spoke against it: yet such was repeatedly the case.

Their recent reverses had but led the people at Mbau to the more eager pursuit of war; and to this every thing had to yield. While heathen temples were being rebuilt with new zeal in the hope of propitiating the gods who had deceived them, they had but little time or inclination to erect a mission house: so the hope of an establishment here was again deferred.

In 1852 the old king, Tanoa, died. It was

not often that any one was allowed to live so long: but Thakombau would never listen to any proposition to put his father to death.

The death of the king had been looked forward to by the missionaries with great interest. If Thakombau could be induced to prevent the strangling of the women, and the custom thus be once broken through, it would be felt throughout Fiji; while the failure of their earnest efforts to bring about this result would confirm the custom. As the king daily grew weaker, the missionaries became more urgent, warning the chief of the enormity of the crime contemplated. Besides an offering of whales' teeth to redeem the victims, Mr. Calvert, in Fijian style, offered to have a finger cut off if they could be spared.

Thakombau was respectful, but resolute in his determination to obey the custom of ages and honor his father in the usual manner. He told the missionaries which women would be killed, and asked them to visit them. They did so, and found them fully resolved to die.

The horrible scene which occurred is thus described:—

On the 6th of December Mr. Calvert was called away to Ovalau. The next day Mr. Watsford went to Mbau alone, and found all the women at the king's house weeping. The selected victims were pointed out, with their friends weeping over them; and he warned them faithfully of the punishment that awaited the wicked in another world,— to which one of them boldly answered, "Who fears hell-fire? We shall jump in there the day the king dies." Passing into the principal house, he was still more shocked to see Thakombau's wife and some more women preparing the dresses for the others to wear on the day of their death. Mr. Watsford went to the young king, and found him among his assembled chiefs, where once more the solemn warnings were faithfully spoken; but in vain. The missionary then returned to Viwa, but soon crossed over again to Mbau, where he remained till midnight, trying to save the women. Before leaving, he backed his last appeal by offering the new whale-boat belonging to the mission, twenty muskets, and all his own personal property; but still in vain. Early the next morning he went back to Mbau, and found that Tanoa was dead. Hastening on to the house where he lay, Mr. Watsford saw six biers standing at the door,—from which he knew that *five* victims, at least, were to accompany their dead lord to the grave.

Within the house the work of death was begun. One woman was already strangled, and the second was kneeling with covered head, while several men on either side were just pulling the cord which wound round her neck, when the missionary stood on the threshold, heart-sick and faint at the ghastly sight. Soon the woman fell dead. Mr. Watsford knew her. She had professed Christianity, and shrunk from death, asking to go to prayer. But, when the fatal moment came, she arose when called, and, passing the old king's corpse, spat on it, saying, "Ah, you old wretch! I shall be in hell with you directly!" The third was now called for, when Thakombau caught sight of the missionary, and, trembling with fear, looked at him in agony and cried out, "What about it, Mr. Watsford?"

Mr. Watsford with great difficulty answered, "Refrain, sir! That is plenty. Two are dead. Refrain! I love them!"

The chief replied, "We also love them. They are not many,—only five. But for you missionaries, many more would have been strangled."

Just then a third victim approached, who had offered to die instead of her sister, who had a son living. She had sat impatiently, and, on hearing her name, started up instantly. She was a fine woman, of high rank, and wore a new *liku*. Looking proudly around on the people seated in the apartment, she pranced up to the place of death, offering her hand to Mr. Watsford, who shrank back in disgust. When about to kneel, she saw that they were going to use a shabby cord, and haughtily refused to be strangled except with a new cord. All this time the assembly gazed at her with delight, gently clapping their hands, and expressing, in subdued exclamations, their admiration of her beauty and pride. She then bade her relatives farewell, and knelt down, with her arms round one of her friends. The cord was adjusted and the large covering thrown over her; and while the men strained the cord a woman of rank pressed down the head of the poor wretch, who died without a sound or struggle. Two more followed.

Throughout the terrible scene there was no noise or excitement; but a cheerful composure seemed to possess every one there, except Thakombau, who was much excited, and evidently making a great effort to act his murderous part before the face of God's messenger. He ordered that one of the victims should live; but she refused; and her own son helped the king and the rest to strangle her. Mr. Watsford, by painful effort, stayed to the last, protesting against the heartless butchery which he and his brethren had so long striven to prevent.

During a war which took place with Ovalau in 1853, Thakombau was seriously embarrassed by a tribe of mountaineers who revolted from their allegiance. Elijah Verani,—once the brutal heathen chief, now a preacher of the gospel,—ever faithful to his friend, offered to go and, if possible, win them back. Mr. Calvert remonstrated with him on account of the danger of the undertaking; but Verani was resolute. He had sent messengers, who were not allowed to land; and the only course open to him was to go himself. On leaving, he said, "This may be the time of my removal."

With a small party, he went on his perilous mission. It seemed at first likely to be successful. The chiefs received him and his gifts graciously; but when the Lakemba king heard of his arrival he offered his sister and some property as a bribe to the mountaineers if they would kill Verani. The bribe was accepted; and the next morning, as Elijah and his party were walking past a temple, they were fired upon. A man then ran at Elijah with a club; but the Viwan chief wrested it from him and threw it on the ground. The man again seized it, and his victim could offer no more resistance: a ball had struck him, and he fell dead beneath the blows of the club. All the party but one perished, and several were eaten, among whom was a valuable preacher. The bodies of Elijah, his two brothers, and another were taken to Levuka, where the murderers received liberal payment from the whites and the natives. Mr. Waterhouse went boldly and begged for the bodies, which were given up to him and decently buried.

Such was the end of the renowned Verani, the Christian chief Elijah. He who before his conversion had put so many to a violent death at last fell by the hands of murderers.

The death of his friend produced a powerful impression upon Thakombau, who had suffered humiliations and reverses of late, and whose influence was resisted by an organized opposition in the islands.

He was led by these events to consent that a missionary should reside in Mbau, and gave up a small stone house for his use. Mr. Waterhouse went immediately.

Soon afterwards Thakombau was attacked by severe illness; and the thought of approaching death was terrible to him. While he was in this state, the news of the assassination of Tui Thakau, King of Somo-somo, was brought him. Mr. Calvert told him that this chief had been long and faithfully warned by the servants of God, but had resisted the truth, and was now suddenly cut off without hope of salvation. "And does the Lord work so?" he anxiously asked. Mr. Calvert answered him that he did, and that he too had been warned, and should seek the mercy of God before it should be too late.

Thakombau seemed much softened by these events. After much deliberation and hesitancy, he made up his mind to publicly profess his change of faith.

Mr. Calvert came from Ovalau to conduct the services. At nine o'clock the death-drum—*rongo-rongoi valu* (reporter of war)—was beaten. Ten days before, its sound had called the people together to a cannibal feast; now it gave the signal for assembling in the great Stranger's House for the worshipping of the true God. About three hundred people were in the building, before whom stood the chief with his children and many wives and other relatives. In front of him was his priest,—an old man with gray hair and a long beard. All had assumed the more ample *lotu* dress, and were well-behaved and serious. Mr. Calvert, who had so long watched and toiled for this event, was deeply moved by the scene, and could scarcely find voice to go on with the service. That was a day ever to be remembered as one of the most important in the annals of Fiji. After worship the people crowded about the missionaries to ask for alphabets, and gathered in groups to learn to read. In the afternoon Mr. Waterhouse preached to a congregation as large as that of the morning.

Thakombau was evidently relieved, now that he had thrown off the old yoke of heathenism. He caused the Sabbath to be strictly observed, and procured a large bell by which to summon his numerous household to family prayer. His own attendance at the preaching and prayer-meetings was regular, and his deportment serious. His little boy of about seven years of age had already been permitted to bear the name of Christian, and had learned to read. The little fellow now became the teacher of his parents, who were both so eager to acquire knowledge that sometimes their young instructor would fall asleep with fatigue in the midst of the lesson, to resume it after a refreshing nap.

The king's example was followed by many, —some from motives of expediency, and others from sincere conviction.

The change in Thakombau was not as yet a very vital one. His judgment was convinced, but his heart did not yield, and the principles of heathenism were not altogether uprooted from his soul.

Ratu Nggara, the Rewan chief, elated by his own recent successes and the reverses of his rival, sent word to Mr. Waterhouse to remove from Mbau, because he was about to destroy the town and its king. This the missionary refused to do, regarding the threatened danger as making his presence more needful. Thakombau was surprised and touched by this, and said, "When the vessel is sinking, every one is anxious to provide for his own safety,—as many of my own relatives are doing; but you, when I am reviled, remain to perish with me."

"Only be faithful to God and follow the guidance of his word, and I will remain with you until your death, should it be permitted to come to pass during the present agitation," replied Mr. Waterhouse.

Every day the troubles and dangers of Mbau became more threatening. The cause of religion was aided rather than hindered by this, however; for the people and their king sought after God in their distress, and Thakombau's proud heart melted under the pressure of grief and anxiety, until he sat at the feet of Jesus to learn of him endurance and forgiveness of enemies.

He sent to the Rewan king, proposing peace. The king, thinking that this was a token of weakness, sent back a proud refusal,—saying that he would soon kill and eat Thakombau, and that he defied his God Jehovah to save him from his vengeance. The humble chief had now calm confidence in God, and could hear this message unmoved.

A spy was detected in an effort to bribe a town of Mbau to revolt. He was sent safely back to Rewa, wearing a new dress given him by Thakombau.

During these difficulties the missionaries endeavored to keep on peaceable terms with both parties. They went constantly from one to the other, and were often in circumstances of very great danger in making these journeys. The God whom they served was truly, however, "their shield and buckler" in all these days of peril.

The dreaded war was prevented by the death of the Rewan king, Ratu Nggara. When Thakombau heard of this event, he immediately sent to Rewa, asking for peace. "Tell the Rewa people," said he, "to become Christian, and let us establish a peace that shall be lasting. If we fight and one party conquers, thereby making peace, evil will remain and spring up. Let us all become Christian and establish peace: then all will be likely to go on well. I am Christian, not because I am weak or afraid, but because I know it to be true. I trust in God alone."

The chiefs received this message favorably, and sent an ambassador to Mbau with a peace-offering. This war and peace have already been referred to in our chapter on Rewa.

The work of the missionaries, after much toil and discouragement, was thus followed by success at last. The great Stranger's House at Mbau was set apart for the public worship of God, and about a thousand people would meet there, a large proportion of whom were evidently sincere worshippers,—many of them having bitterly repented of their sins and brought forth fruits meet for repentance. The great centre being gained, the good work went on without hindrance on all hands. Chapels were built and houses opened for religious service in every direction.

Mr. Calvert left Fiji in 1855, after having spent seventeen years in active labor there. He returned to England to superintend the printing of the Bible in Fijian. The Sunday before he left the islands, he preached to a crowded congregation in the Stranger's House. The memory of what Mbau once was, the sight of its present condition, gratitude to God for the success with which he had at last crowned their toil and suffering, moved the missionary's heart most deeply; nor were the congregation before him unaffected by the occasion.

In 1857, Thakombau was married to his queen. His numerous other wives were sent away; and with them he sacrificed more wealth and influence than can be estimated by strangers to Fijian life. This act, therefore, was a most convincing proof of the change Christianity had wrought in him.

The hindrance to his baptism was now removed, and the rite was performed January 11, 1857. In the afternoon the king was publicly baptized. In the presence of God, he promised to "renounce the devil and all his works, the pomps and vanities of this wicked world, and the sinful lusts of the flesh." He then addressed the assembly. It must have cost him many a struggle to stand up before his court, his ambassadors, and the flower of his people, to confess his former sins. In time past he had considered himself a god, and had received honors almost divine from his people; now he humbles himself and adores his great Creator and merciful Preserver.

And what a congregation he had! Husbands whose wives he had dishonored! widows whose husbands he had slain! sisters whose relatives had been strangled by his orders! relatives whose friends he had eaten! and children the descendants of those he had murdered, and who had vowed to avenge the wrongs inflicted on their fathers!

A thousand stony hearts heaved with fear and astonishment as Thakombau gave utterance to the following sentiments:—"I have been a bad man. I disturbed the country. The missionaries came and invited me to embrace Christianity; but I said to them, 'I will continue to fight.' God has singularly preserved my life. At one time I thought that I had myself been the instrument of my own preservation; but now I know that it was the Lord's doing. I desire to acknowledge him as the only and the true God. I have scourged the world." He was deeply affected, and spoke with great diffidence.

The work now entered upon a new life. Soon in the Mbau district alone the attendants on Christian worship numbered ten thousand.

CONCLUSION.

In looking over this sketch of Fijian mission history, the magnitude of the work accomplished must strike the thoughtful mind, and the devout heart cannot but humbly say, "Be thou exalted, Lord! we will sing and praise thy power." The change wrought in Fiji could never have been brought to pass by human strength or wisdom. God has been working in those savage natures. In parts of these islands he has caused cannibalism, polygamy, infanticide, authorized murders, and brutal despotism to fade away almost to extinction. He has caused civilization to advance with slow but steady steps towards full development. There is still darkness, superstition, misery, and crime marring the beauty of these fair islands and mingling a wail with the song of praise which arises from those who have been redeemed to God. The urgent, pleading call for more missionaries in Fiji comes from thousands who would hear if one were there to speak to them, and from the weary, overburdened laborers who are *willing* to work till they lie down exhausted to die, but who might fulfil their measure of duties for years to come if there were but men enough to share their toil and their reward. Let the prayers of Christians ascend before the throne of the Great King until the Islands of the Sea shall all bow at his feet.

THE END.

www.ingramcontent.com/pod-product-compliance
Lightning Source LLC
Chambersburg PA
CBHW032016220426
43664CB00006B/271